Ma

DIRECTIONS

WRITTEN AND RESEARCHED BY

Phil Lee

ROUGH GUIDES

NEW YORK • LONDON • DELHI

www.roughguides.com

Contents

Introduction   4

Ideas   9

The big six.................................10
Restaurants 12
Churches and shrines.......................14
Festivals 16
Caves and castles..........................18
Clubbers' Palma 20
Prehistoric and Roman Mallorca 22
Birdwatchers' Mallorca....................24
Monastery rooms...........................26
Gastronomic Mallorca......................28
The Mallorcan Primitives 30
Beaches 32
Town and city hotels.......................34
Rural and resort hotels 36
Mallorcan wine.............................38
Kids' Mallorca..............................40
Green Mallorca 42
Sports.....................................44
Modern art in Mallorca 46

Places   49

Palma......................................51
The Bay of Palma 74
Western Mallorca...........................84
Northern Mallorca.........................106
Southern Mallorca 125

Essentials   149

Arrival...................................151
Information and websites 152
Maps......................................153
Transport 153
Accommodation.............................155
Sports and activities 156
Festivals 156
Directory.................................158

Language   161

Index   188

Introduction to

Mallorca

Commonly perceived as little more than sun, sex, booze and high-rise hotels, Mallorca is – to the surprise of many first–time visitors – often beautiful and frequently fascinating. The island's negative image was spawned by the helter-skelter development of the 1960s, which submerged tracts of the coastline beneath hotels, villas and apartment blocks, but in fact, the concrete

▲ Modernista building

sprawl is largely confined to the Bay of Palma and a handful of mega-resorts, and for the most part Mallorca remains untouched. Another surprise is the startling variety that characterizes the island, from the craggy mountains and medieval monasteries of its northwest coast through to the whitewashed towns and rolling farmland of the central plain – altogether quite enough to attract a battery of artists, actors and writers from Robert Graves to Michael Douglas.

Mallorca is the largest of the Balearic islands, an archipelago to the east of the Spanish mainland comprising four main islands

▲ Church of Nostra Senyora de la Esperança, Capdepera

▲ Estellencs

– Mallorca, Menorca, Ibiza and Formentera. As such, it straddled the sailing routes between the east and west Mediterranean, and was an important and prosperous trading station until the sixteenth century, when the Spanish dash to exploit the Americas turned trade routes on their heads. Thereafter, the island became a neglected Mediterranean backwater controlled by a conservative landed gentry, whose large estates dominated Es Pla, the fertile central plain, until mass tourism simply swept the established order away in the 1960s. Agriculture, once the mainstay of the local economy, faded into the background, and the island's former poverty evaporated: today, Mallorca's population of 640,000 enjoys the highest per capita level of disposable income in Spain.

Catalan and Castilian

After the death of Franco in 1975, Spain was divided on federal lines with the Balearics forming their own autonomous region. One result was the re-emergence of Catalan (*Català*), the main language of the islanders, at the expense of Castilian (Spanish), which Franco had imposed as the only language of government and education. The most obvious sign of this linguistic change has been the replacement of Castilian street names by their Catalan equivalents. The islanders speak Catalan in a local dialect, *Mallorquín*, though they are almost all bilingual, speaking Castilian and Catalan with equal fluency.

▼ Coves d'Artà

When to visit

Spring and autumn are the ideal times for a visit, when the weather is comfortably warm with none of the oven-like temperatures which bake the island in July and August. It's well worth considering a winter break too: even in January, temperatures are usually high enough during the day to sit out at a café in shirtsleeves. Mallorca sees occasional rain in winter, and the Serra de Tramuntana mountains, which protect the rest of Mallorca from inclement weather and the prevailing northerly winds, are often buffeted by storms.

Mallorca
AT A GLANCE

PALMA

Palma, the island capital, arches around the shores of the Bay of Palma. It is the Balearics' one real city, a bustling, historic place whose grandee mansions and magnificent Gothic cathedral serve as a fine backdrop to an excellent café and restaurant scene.

▲ Illetes beach

▲ Old town, Palma

home and studio of Joan Miró in Cala Major and the cove beach of Portals Vells.

WESTERN MALLORCA

The wild and wonderful Serra de Tramuntana mountains bump along the island's northwest coastline, punctuated by deep sheltered valleys, mountain villages and beautiful cove beaches. Roughly midway is Sóller, an old market town, which is best reached from Palma on the antique railway, an extraordinarily scenic journey.

THE BAY OF PALMA (BADIA DE PALMA)

The tourist resorts to either side of Palma combine in a thirty-kilometre-long stretch of intensive development that can be dispiriting. Nevertheless, there are highlights, principally the former

NORTHERN MALLORCA

Beyond Sóller, the Serra de Tramuntana mountains thunder

▶ Serres Tramuntana

along the coastline as far as Lluc monastery before rolling down to a coastal plain, which holds the lovely little town of Pollença, the attractive resort of Port de Pollença and a key birdwatching site; the Parc Natural de S'Albufera.

SOUTHERN MALLORCA

East of Palma stretches Es Pla, an agricultural plain that occupies the centre of the island, sprinkled with country towns, most memorably Petra and Sineu. In the east, Es Pla is bounded by Mallorca's second mountain range, the gentler Serres de Llevant, which runs just inland from the mega-resorts, coves and caves of the east coast and culminates in the pine-clad headlands and medieval hill towns of the island's northeast corner. The sparse flatlands of the south coast are less appealing, but Colònia de Sant Jordi is an agreeable resort and home port for the boat to Cabrera island.

▶ Serres de Llevant

Ideas

The big six

Mallorca has lots of hidden corners and a staggeringly beautiful shoreline as well as some outstanding individual sights. Two are monasteries, Lluc and Valldemossa, where Chopin and his lover, George Sand, spent the winter of 1838, and another is the magnificent Gothic extravagance of Palma Cathedral. There's also the train over the mountains between Palma and Sóller, the mountain village of Deià and the sun-bleached mountains themselves, the Serra de Tramuntana.

▲ **The Palma to Sóller train**

This antique train provides a fine introduction to Mallorca's mountainous charms.

P.86 ▶ WESTERN MALLORCA

▲ **Palma Cathedral**

The capital's most impressive building, Palma Cathedral is quite simply one of Spain's finest Gothic buildings.

P.51 ▶ PALMA

▲ Deià

Of all the mountain villages strung along the northwest coast, Deià is probably the prettiest.

P.93 ▸ WESTERN MALLORCA

▼ Monestir de Lluc

Hidden in the mountains, Lluc holds La Morenata – the Black Madonna – the island's holiest icon.

P.109 ▸ NORTHERN MALLORCA

▲ Valldemossa Monastery

Amongst the island's monasteries, Valldemossa is the most enchanting and the prior's cell is stuffed with objets d'art.

P.97 ▸ WESTERN MALLORCA

▶ Serra de Tramuntana

This range of rugged mountains bands the northwest coast and makes for ideal hiking in the spring and autumn.

P.106 ▸ WESTERN MALLORCA

Restaurants

Several million tourists land on Mallorca every year, one result being a superabundance of restaurants. Standards vary enormously, but almost every resort, town and village has at least a couple of good places and there's also a scattering of memorable restaurants dotted right across the island, nowhere more so than in Palma. The best restaurants often make use of local produce with seafood, pig and lamb leading the gastronomic way.

▲ Es Parlament

One of the capital's fanciest restaurants with an excellent line in paella.

P.71 ▸ PALMA

▲ El Guía

Traditional restaurant in Sóller offering a first-rate *menú del día*.

P.102 ▸ WESTERN MALLORCA

▼ Ca'n Mario

Family-run, first-floor restaurant offering traditional island food at very reasonable prices.

P.103 ▶ WESTERN MALLORCA

▲ Es Racó d'es Teix

Wonderful views and wonderful food at this top-flight Deià restaurant.

P.104 ▶ WESTERN MALLORCA

▼ Ca'n Carlos

Outstanding restaurant in the centre of Palma featuring the best of Mallorcan cuisine.

P.71 ▶ PALMA

Churches and shrines

Profoundly Catholic for much of its history, Mallorca possesses literally scores of churches and a scattering of hilltop shrines, where the penitential still troop off for blessings and cures. Most of the more important churches are Gothic in design, dating from the thirteenth and fourteenth centuries, but their interiors are largely Baroque, adorned by kitsch – or mawkish – religious statues and paintings.

▲ Palma Cathedral

Overlooking the Mediterranean, the Cathedral is the most impressive church on the island by a long chalk.

P.51 ▶ PALMA

▲ Basílica de Sant Francesc, Palma

Built for the Franciscans, this church has all manner of Gothic and Baroque details.

P.61 ▶ PALMA

▼ Santa Eulalia, Palma

Classic Gothic church dating from the thirteenth century and with a colossal high altar

P.60 ▸ PALMA

▼ Nostra Senyora Verge dels Dolors, Manacor

Well-proportioned Gothic church overlooking the town's main square.

P.131 ▸ SOUTHERN MALLORCA

▲ Santuari de Nostra Senyora de Cura, Puig Randa

Dinky little church perched on a hill and part of a complex that was formerly a Franciscan monastery.

P.128 ▸ SOUTHERN MALLORCA

▼ Nostra Senyora de los Angeles, Sineu

The grandest parish church on the island with a mighty freestanding bell tower.

P.129 ▸ SOUTHERN MALLORCA

Festivals

Almost every town and village in Mallorca takes at least one day off a year to devote to a festival. Usually it's the local saint's day, but there are celebrations, too, of harvests, deliverance from the Moors, of safe return from the sea – any excuse will do. Each festival is, of course, different, with a particular local emphasis, but there is always music, dancing, traditional costume and an immense spirit of enjoyment.

▲ Sa Firá I Es Firó

A life-saving victory by the inhabitants of Sóller over invading Turks is commemorated with mock battles in mid-May.

P.157 ▶ ESSENTIALS

▲ Corpus Christi

Early to mid-June, dances and processions in several of the island's towns – here in Sóller.

P.157 ▶ ESSENTIALS

▶ Carnaval (Carnival)

Marches and fancy dress parades in every Mallorcan town during the week before Lent – in February.

P.157 ▶
ESSENTIALS

17

▼ Revetla de Sant Antoni Abat (Eve of St Antony's Day)

Masks and parties and the lighting of bonfires across the island mark this saint's day, on January 16.

P.156 ▶ ESSENTIALS

▲ Escolania de Lluc

The choir boys of Lluc monastery perform at mass twice daily – usually at 11am and 7pm.

P.109 ▶ WESTERN MALLORCA

▼ Setmana Santa (Holy Week)

During Easter week the island sees dozens of religious ceremonies – like this ominous-looking parade in Palma.

P.157 ▶ ESSENTIALS

Caves and castles

Dating back to Moorish times, Mallorca's hilltop castles fascinated the Victorians, who explored their every nook and cranny. They also had a penchant for the limestone cave systems of eastern Mallorca. There are three main ones to choose from, but the most enjoyable is perhaps the 450m-long series of caverns that comprise the Coves d'Artà.

▲ Castell de Bellver, Palma

Dating from the fourteenth century, this hilltop castle is in immaculate condition and offers stirring views over Palma.

P.66 ▶ PALMA

▲ Capdepera

Postcard-perfect castle whose castellated walls clamber up the steepest of hillsides.

P.134 ▶ NORTHERN MALLORCA

▲ Castell d'Alaró

The shattered ruins of this former Moorish stronghold occupy a stupendously wild location.

P.91 ▸ WESTERN MALLORCA

▼ Castell de Santueri

Long abandoned, the crumbling stonework of this medieval fortress glowers across the surrounding flatlands.

P.139 ▸ SOUTHERN MALLORCA

▲ Coves d'Artà

The yawning caverns of the Coves d'Artà attract visitors by the hundred.

P.135 ▸ SOUTHERN MALLORCA

Clubbers' Palma

Every resort in every part of the island has a healthy supply of bars and restaurants, but only in Palma does the nightlife really hum, with a clutch of lively bars and nightclubs. Here in the capital, there's something to suit every disposition, whether straight or gay, budget or expense account.

▲ **Tito's, Palma**
Established nightspot playing every sort of music, plus frequent live bands.

P.72 ▶ PALMA

▼ DJ events

Palma offers regular musical
spectaculars with well-known DJs
often appearing outside at the Parc
de la Mar.

P.57 ▶ PALMA

▶ Abaco, Palma

Ambitious late-night bar bedecked in
flowers and serving fanciful cocktails.

P.71 ▶ PALMA

▼ Pacha, Palma

Several bars and loud house and
techno music define this popular club.

P.72 ▶ PALMA

Prehistoric and Roman Mallorca

Mallorca is dotted with prehistoric remains, a remarkably varied bunch mostly dating from around 1400 to 800 BC. There are colonies of cave dwellings overlooking the ocean, underground halls and chambers, cone-shaped rock mounds – *talayots* – that may have been watchtowers, and several walled villages, most memorably Ses Paisses. The Romans occupied Mallorca in 146 BC and stayed for nearly six hundred years. Little remains from this period, but there are two noteworthy sights at Alcúdia.

▲ Pollentia, Alcúdia

Roman Pollentia was once an important trading station and colony.

P.117 ▶ NORTHERN MALLORCA

▲ Prehistoric monuments

Mallorca is dotted with prehistoric remains holding ruined mounds and walls, plus the occasional underground chamber.

P.132 ▶ SOUTHERN MALLORCA

▼ Teatre Roman, Alcúdia

This open-air theatre is the most rewarding of the island's Roman remains.

P.117 ▶ NORTHERN MALLORCA

▼ Capocorb Vell

The sprawling ruins of this prehistoric village hold no less than five stone towers, or *talayots*.

P.145 ▶ SOUTHERN MALLORCA

▲ Ses Paisses, Artà

Ses Paisses is the best-preserved prehistoric settlement on Mallorca and comes complete with its cyclopean walls.

P.132 ▶ SOUTHERN MALLORCA

Birdwatchers' Mallorca

Mallorca's diverse birdlife has attracted ornithologists for decades. The island boasts a whole batch of resident Mediterranean specialists plus migrating flocks of North European birds which arrive in their thousands during the spring and autumn. The northern mountains are a haven for birds of prey, the cliffs of the western coast are thronged with seabirds, the island's country lanes have corn buntings, warblers, nightingales and hoopoes, and the island's wetlands attract a varied crew from moorhens and crakes to raptors.

▲ Hoopoe (Upupa epops)

Pigeon-sized, pinky-brown bird with barred head-crest and wings; breeding resident favouring open ground, for example at Mondragó.

P.140 ▸ SOUTHERN MALLORCA

▲ Purple Gallinule (Porphyrio porphyrio)

Strange purple-blue, hen-like bird, which is a breeding resident at the Parc Natural de S'Albufera.

P.119 ▸ NORTHERN MALLORCA

CAP BLAU — ANADE REAL MALLARD STOCKENTE
ANAS PLATYRHYNCHOS

SIULADOR — ANADE SILBON WIGEON PFEIFENTE
ANAS PENELOPE

▲ Cap de Formentor

This cape is the breeding ground of shear-waters, Mediterranean shag, storm petrels and Audouin's Gull.

P.115 ▶ NORTHERN MALLORCA

▼ Black Vulture (Aegypius monachus)

The most distinctive of the island's birds, this solitary raptor is a breeding resident confined to the northern mountains.

P.106 ▶ NORTHERN MALLORCA

▼ Audoin's Gull (Larus audouinii)

A rare gull, with an unusual red bill, this resident breeder sticks to rocky stretches of coastline, like the Formentor peninsula.

P.115 ▶ NORTHERN MALLORCA

▼ Parc Natural de S'Albufera

The wetlands here are the best birdwatch-ing spot on the island; the park has a dozen hides.

P.119 ▶ NORTHERN MALLORCA

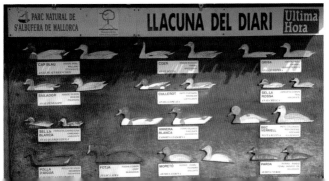

Monastery rooms

Mallorca is short of monks, so short in fact that the monasteries of yesteryear are now maintained by secular wardens, who rent out empty cells at five of them to tourists (of either sex). All have lovely rural settings, four (the exception is Lluc) perch on hilltops and, although there's an increasing demand for this sort of plain and inexpensive accommodation, they are rarely full. Reasonably priced food is usually available at these monasteries, but check when you book.

▲ Monestir de Lluc

The most visited and commercialised of the monasteries providing accommodation, Lluc is also a major tourist attraction.

P.122 ▶ NORTHERN MALLORCA

▲ Ermita de Nostra Senyora de Bonany, near Petra

No frills perhaps, but this monastery is certainly off the beaten track.

P.145 ▶ SOUTHERN MALLORCA

▲ Santuari de Sant Salvador, near Felanitx

Grand views over the east coast and a handsome setting make the Santuari an appealing proposition.

P.146 ▸ SOUTHERN MALLORCA

▼ Santuari de Nostra Senyora de Cura, on Puig Randa, near Algaida

Simple rooms are available in this hilltop complex, which mostly dates from the early twentieth century.

P.146 ▸ SOUTHERN MALLORCA

▲ Ermita de Nostra Senyora del Puig, outside Pollença

With panoramic views over the coastline, this old monastery enjoys a spectacular setting.

P.121 ▸ NORTHERN MALLORCA

Gastronomic Mallorca

Traditional Mallorcan food is a peasant cuisine whose hearty soups and stews, seafood dishes and spiced meats can be delicious. After many years of neglect, it has recently experienced something of a Renaissance and nowadays restaurants offering *Cuina Mallorquína* are comparatively commonplace and should not be missed. Similarly appealing are the island's pastry shops (*pastisserias*), where you'll find the sweetest of confections.

▲ Frito mallorquín

Pigs' offal, potatoes and onions cooked with oil; not for the faint-hearted.

P.171 ▶ LANGUAGE

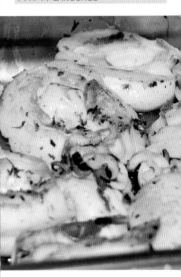

▲ Seafood

Fish (*peix*) and shellfish (*marisc*) are a Mallorcan speciality – from cod to octopus.

P.171 ▶ LANGUAGE

▼ Botifarra

The islanders are extremely partial to spicy
blood sausages (*botifarra*).

P.171 ▶ LANGUAGE

▲ Pa amb oli

An island favourite comprising bread rubbed
with olive oil and eaten with ham, cheese
or fruit.

P.170 ▶ LANGUAGE

▼ Ensaimada

The island's gastronomic pride and joy
is the spiralled flaky pastry known as an
ensaimada.

P.171 ▶ LANGUAGE

The Mallorcan Primitives

The "Mallorcan Primitives" was a school of painters that flourished on the island in the fourteenth and fifteenth centuries. Their output was entirely religious in subject, strikingly naive devotional paintings worked in bold colours on wooden panels. Examples of most of the leading artists of the school are displayed in Palma at the Museu de Mallorca, the Cathedral and the Museu Diocesà.

▲ Francesc Comes (1379–1415)

Comes is noted for his subtle skin textures; this painting is in Palma's church of Santa Eulalia.

P.60 ▶ PALMA

▲ Master of the Privileges

This Master's *Sant Eulalia*, in Palma cathedral, illustrates the suffering of the eponymous saint in ecstatic detail.

P.55 ▶ PALMA

▼ Joan Desi

Desi's *Panel of La Almoina* in Palma Cathedral shows St Francis at the side of Christ.

P.55 ▶ PALMA

▲ Master of Montesión

This unidentified artist looked to his Catalan contemporaries for his sense of movement and tight draughtsmanship.

P.59 ▶ PALMA

Beaches

For all its diverse charms, the main island activity – or lack of it – is sunbathing on the beach. The finest sandy beaches are in the north fringing Port d'Alcúdia and Port de Pollença, on the east coast at Cala Millor, and most fashionably – or skimpily – at the Platja de Palma outside Palma. Meanwhile, the rockier northwest coast is home to a string of cove beaches, almost invariably of shingle and pebble.

▲ Cala Estellencs, Estellencs

This rocky cove beach enjoys a dramatic mountain setting on the northwest coast.

P.100 ▶ WESTERN MALLORCA

▲ Port d'Alcúdia

Honest, there ain't no crocodiles here – and the safe and sandy beach gently shelves into the ocean.

P.118 ▶ NORTHERN MALLORCA

▲ Cala Deià, Deià

Sand is in short supply here, but the rugged mountain setting on the northwest coast is handsome compensation.

P.93 ▸ WESTERN MALLORCA

▶ Es Trenc

The best beach on the south coast, this long, sandy strand is largely – and surprisingly – undeveloped.

P.142 ▸ SOUTHERN MALLORCA

◀ Platja de Palma

Bronzed and oiled bodies throng this popular beach, which is flanked by a seemingly interminable string of beach-gear shops.

P.76 ▸ BAY OF PALMA

▶ Mondragó

Now safely ensconced within a nature conservation area, Mondragó has escaped crass development.

P.140 ▸ SOUTHERN MALLORCA

Town and city hotels

Ten years ago, there were hardly any hotels inland from the coast – even a popular little town like Pollença had only one or two. Things are very different now with almost all of Mallorca's larger settlements, and especially Palma, equipped with a hatful of hotels, and oftentimes they occupy immaculately renovated old stone houses, which were formerly the homes of the island's upper crust.

▲ Hotel Portixol, Es Portixol

Urbane, "boutique" hotel sporting all sorts of fancy designer details; 2km east of Palma Cathedral.

P.83 ▸ BAY OF PALMA

▲ Hotel Saratoga, Palma

Bright and breezy, seven-storey modern hotel with spick-and-span balconied rooms – and this rooftop café.

P.68 ▸ PALMA

▼ Hotel El Guía, Sóller

Unassuming but full of character, this long-established, one-star hotel is metres from Sóller train station.

P.102 ▸ WESTERN MALLORCA

▼ Scott's Binissalem, Binissalem

One of the classiest hotels around, with each room kitted out in immaculate taste and style.

P.103 ▸ WESTERN MALLORCA

▲ Hotel-residencia Born, Palma

Traditional, even old-fashioned, hotel set in a rambling old town house with an attractive, leafy courtyard.

P.68 ▸ PALMA

Rural and resort hotels

The burgeoning demand for rural, rustic holidays has spawned several dozen country hotels, mostly located in or near the mountainous northwest coast. Some are solitary affairs, surrounded by olive and almond groves, others are in little villages and most occupy tastefully renovated old farm and merchants' houses. These rural hotels are, however, small beer compared to the superabundance of resort hotels, which range from humble little places to mammoth tower blocks with a number of delightful hotels in between.

▲ Hotel Formentor

One of the island's first deluxe hotels, the *Formentor* occupies a splendid 1920s building in an equally splendid coastal setting.

P.121 ▸ NORTHERN MALLORCA

▲ Hotel Ca's Xorc, near Sóller

Charming hotel in a creatively revamped old olive mill set among the mountains outside Sóller.

P.102 ▶ WESTERN MALLORCA

▼ Hotel Costa d'Or, near Deià

The *Costa d'Or* has several virtues, but its superb coastal location, high above the ocean, is well-nigh unbeatable.

P.102 ▶ WESTERN MALLORCA

▲ Scott's Galilea

One of the island's most satisfying hotels, located in the mountain hamlet of Galilea.

P.103 ▶ WESTERN MALLORCA

Mallorcan wine

In the 1990s, a concerted effort was made to raise the quality of Mallorcan wine. The results have been tremendously successful and Mallorca has now been granted two Denominació d'Origen (DO) credentials – DO wines, with their quality guarantees, being the best in Spain. One Mallorcan DO is Binissalem, named after a small, wine-producing town near Palma, the other is Pla i Llevant, which refers to a much larger area in the centre of the island.

▲ Festa d'es Verema, Binissalem

The Festival of the Grape Harvest is celebrated with gusto in Binissalem; don't wear your Sunday suit.

P.92 ▸ WESTERN MALLORCA

▲ Herederos de Ribas Binissalem Blanco

Herederos de Ribas produces Mallorca's best white wines; this version is lively and fruity.

P.92 ▸ WESTERN MALLORCA

▲ Bodega José Ferrer, Binissalem

The José Ferrer brand denotes Mallorca's most satisfying red wines.

P.92 ▸ WESTERN MALLORCA

▼ José Ferrer Red Binissalem

A fine local vintage, Red Binissalem is a robust and aromatic wine made predominantly from the *mantonegro* grape.

P.92 ▸ WESTERN MALLORCA

▲ Casa del Vino, Manacor

Specialist wine shops are springing up all over the island and this is one of the best.

P.148 ▸ SOUTHERN MALLORCA

Kids' Mallorca

Pedaloe-pedalling, paddling, swimming, buckets and sand are quite enough to keep most kids happy for days on end, especially as hotel (and villa) swimming pools are commonplace, but teens may want something a bit more ambitious and Mallorca's themed water parks fit the bill.

▲ Marineland, Portals Nous

Giant tanks and aquaria plus dolphins galore delight many a child.

P.78 ▸ BAY OF PALMA

▲ Aquacity, S'Arenal

Everything watery – from swimming pools to chutes and flumes.

P.76 ▸ BAY OF PALMA

▲ Aquapark, Magaluf

Enormous water park – not the revenge of the whales.

P.79 ▸ BAY OF PALMA

▼ Hidropark, Port d'Alcúdia

An honest-to-goodness water park with pools, flumes and chutes.

P.118 ▸ NORTHERN MALLORCA

▲ Western Water Park, Magaluf

Idiosyncratic mix of water park and Wild West town that gives kitsch a bad name.

P.79 ▸ BAY OF PALMA

Green Mallorca

Not before time perhaps, but in recent years the Balearic government has begun to curtail development and protect its natural environment, creating a string of parks across Mallorca. They are a varied bunch, ranging from wetlands and coast through to uninhabited islets, and Mallorca's green credentials are further supplemented by the large chunks of wilderness – or at least semi-wilderness – that make up much of the Serra de Tramuntana mountains.

▲ Sa Dragonera

Now protected as a nature reserve, this craggy uninhabited islet lies off Mallorca's west coast.

P.100 ▶ WESTERN MALLORCA

▲ Mondragó Parc Natural

This east-coast park is a mixed bag of wetland, farm and scrubland.

P.140 ▶ SOUTHERN MALLORCA

▲ Cap Formentor

Wild and surf-battered cape which remains almost entirely pristine.

P.115 ▶ NORTHERN MALLORCA

▼ Parc Natural de S'Albufera

Scenically, these protected wetlands are hardly heart-stopping, but this is the best birdwatching site on the island.

P.119 ▶ NORTHERN MALLORCA

▲ Serra de Tramuntana

This mountain range runs the length of the island's northwest coast, providing its most memorable scenery.

P.106 ▶ WESTERN MALLORCA & NORTHERN MALLORCA

▼ Gorg Blau

High up in the mountains, the Blue Gorge reservoir enjoys an especially dramatic setting.

P.107 ▶ NORTHERN MALLORCA

Sports

At all the larger resorts, watersports are the big deal and companies line up to hire out equipment for everything from sailing, pedaloe-pedalling, jet skiing and windsurfing through to inflatable gear for learner swimmers. Scuba diving and snorkelling are also commonplace, with the clearest diving around the islet of Illa Dragonera and off Cala Figuera. Equally popular is hiking, with hundreds of hikers descending on the Serra de Tramuntana mountains in the spring and autumn.

▲ **Bóquer valley, near Port de Pollença**

The Bóquer, with its rich birdlife, makes a perfect day's hike from the port.

P.114 ▸ NORTHERN MALLORCA

▲ **Snorkelling**

Snorkel away just about anywhere in Mallorca – this chap is at Port de Sóller.

P.89 ▸ WESTERN MALLORCA

▲ Windsurfing

Windsurfing is popular at many island resorts, especially along the east coast.

P.156 ▶ ESSENTIALS

▼ Jet skiing

Jet skis can be rented at most major resorts.

P.156 ▶ ESSENTIALS

▲ Swimming

Take the plunge into the warm waters of the Med; this diver is at Mondragó.

P.140 ▶ SOUTHERN MALLORCA

Modern art in Mallorca

Mallorca has a strong, indigenous fine-art tradition and has long been a favourite haunt of artists from the Spanish mainland. Pride of artistic place goes to Joan Miró, who had his home and studio in Cala Major, but several other key galleries hold enjoyable and varied assortments of Spanish (and Mallorcan) art, notably the Palau March and the Museu d'Art Espanyol Contemporani in Palma, plus the Museu Municipal Art Contemporani at Valldemossa.

▲ Joan Miró Fundació, Cala Major

The Fundació holds a superb collection of modern art, mostly – but not exclusively – by Joan Miró.

P.77 ▸ BAY OF PALMA

▲ Es Baluard, Palma

A brand-new contemporary-art museum set in an imposing bastion, which was formerly part of the city wall.

P.66 ▸ PALMA

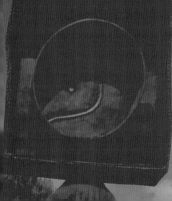

▲ Palau March Museu, Palma

Former mansion, now an enjoyable art museum, whose courtyard features Xavier Corbero's *Orgue del Mar* (Sea Organ).

P.56 ▸ PALMA

▲ Museu Municipal d'Art Contemporani, Valldemossa monastery

The modern Spanish artist Juli Ramis (1909–1990) is well represented here; this canvas is *Dama Blava* (Blue Lady).

P.97 ▸ WESTERN MALLORCA

▶ Museu d'Art Espanyol Contemporani, Palma

This excellent museum, funded by the Juan March Foundation, explores the Spanish contribution to modern art.

P.65 ▸ PALMA

▲ Joan Miró Fundació, Cala Major

The former studio of Joan Miró has been left pretty much unchanged since the artist's death in 1983.

P.77 ▸ BAY OF PALMA

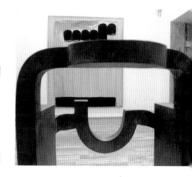

Places

Palma

Palma is a go-ahead and cosmopolitan commercial hub of over 300,000 people. As a major port of call between Europe and North Africa, the city boomed under both Moorish and medieval Christian control, but its wealth and prominence came to a sudden end with the Spanish exploitation of the New World: from the early sixteenth century, Madrid looked west across the Atlantic and Palma slipped into Mediterranean obscurity. With its appointment as the capital of the newly established autonomous region of the Balearics in 1983, the city shed its dusty provincialism and the new-found self-confidence is plain to see. The centre now presents a splendid ensemble of lively shopping areas and refurbished old buildings, mazy lanes, fountains, gardens and sculpture, all enclosed by what remains of the old city walls and their replacement boulevards. Yet, for most visitors, Palma's main appeal is its sheer vitality: at night scores of excellent restaurants offer the best of Spanish, Catalan and Mallorcan cuisine, while the city's cafés buzz with chatter.

PLACES Palma

The Cathedral

April, May & Oct Mon–Fri 10am–5.15pm, Sat 10am–2.15pm; June–Sept Mon–Fri 10am–6.15pm, Sat 10am–2.15pm; Nov–March Mon–Fri 10am–3.15pm, Sat 10am–2.15pm; €3.50. Legend has it that when the invasion force of Jaume I of Aragón and Catalunya stood off Mallorca in 1229, a fierce gale threatened to sink the fleet. The desperate king promised to build a church dedicated to the Virgin Mary if the expedition against the Moors was successful. It was, and Jaume fulfilled his promise, starting construction work the next year. The king had a political point to make too – he built his Cathedral (Sa Seu in Catalan) bang on top of the Great Mosque, inside the old Moorish citadel. As it turned

▼ PALMA CATHEDRAL

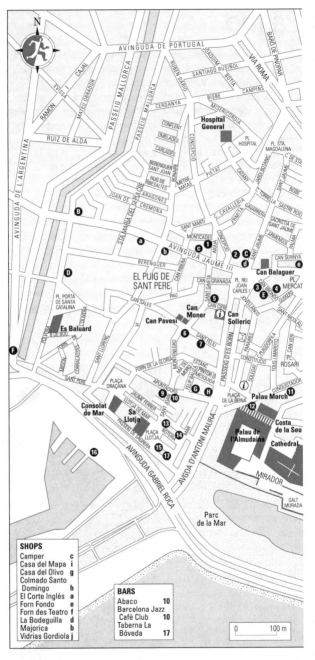

SHOPS

Camper	c
Casa del Mapa	i
Casa del Olivo	g
Colmado Santo Domingo	h
El Corte Inglés	a
Forn Fondo	e
Forn des Teatro	f
La Bodeguilla	d
Majorica	b
Vidrias Gordiola	j

BARS

Abaco	10
Barcelona Jazz	
Café Club	10
Taberna La Bóveda	17

0   100 m

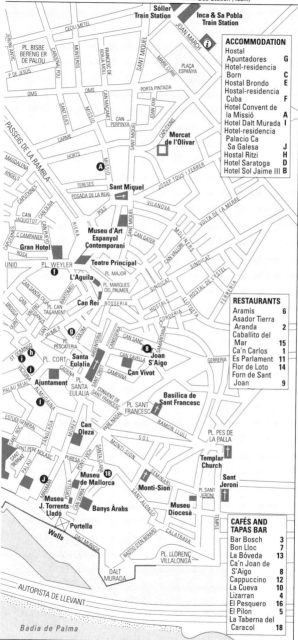

Bus Station (400m)

Sóller Train Station

Inca & Sa Pobla Train Station

ACCOMMODATION

Hostal Apuntadores	G
Hotel-residencia Born	C
Hostal Brondo	E
Hostal-residencia Cuba	F
Hotel Convent de la Missió	A
Hotel Dalt Murada	I
Hotel-residencia Palacio Ca Sa Galesa	J
Hostal Ritzi	H
Hotel Saratoga	D
Hotel Sol Jaime III	B

RESTAURANTS

Aramís	6
Asador Tierra Aranda	2
Caballito del Mar	15
Ca'n Carlos	1
Es Parlament	11
Flor de Loto	14
Forn de Sant Joan	9

CAFÉS AND TAPAS BAR

Bar Bosch	3
Bon Lloc	7
La Bóveda	13
Ca'n Joan de S'Aigo	8
Cappuccino	12
La Cueva	10
Lizarran	4
El Pesquero	16
El Pilon	5
La Taberna del Caracol	18

Badia de Palma

City transport and information

Almost everything of interest in Palma is located in the city centre, a roughly circular affair whose southern perimeter is largely defined by the Cathedral and the remains of the old city walls, which in turn abut the coastal motorway and the harbour. The city centre's landward limits are determined by a zigzag of wide boulevards built beside or in place of the old town walls – Avinguda de la Argentina and Avinguda Gabriel Alomar i Villalonga connect with the coastal motorway, thereby completing the circle. The Via Cintura, the ring road around the suburbs, loops off from the coastal motorway to create a much larger, outer circle. The city centre itself is crossed by four interconnected avenues: Passeig d'es Born, Avinguda Jaume III, c/ Unió (which becomes c/Riera at its eastern end) and Passeig de la Rambla. Your best bet is to use these four thoroughfares to guide yourself round the centre – Palma's jigsaw-like side streets and squares can be very confusing. Central Palma is about 2km in diameter, roughly thirty minutes' walk from one side to the other.

To reach the city's outskirts, take the bus. City buses are operated by EMT (Empresa Municipal de Transports) and almost all their services pass through Plaça Espanya, linking the centre with the suburbs and the nearer tourist resorts. In the city centre, each EMT bus stop sports a large route map with timetable details and neon signs indicating when the next bus is due. Tickets are available from the driver and cost €1.10 per journey within the city limits. A more sedate way of seeing the centre is to take a traditional horse-and-carriage ride from outside the cathedral; count on around €40 for a half-hour jaunt.

There's a provincial tourist office just off Passeig d'es Born at Plaça de la Reina 2 (Mon–Fri 9am–8pm, Sat 9am–2.30pm; ☎971 712216). The main municipal office is inside Can Solleric at Passeig d'es Born 27 (Mon–Fri 9am–8pm, Sat 9am–1.30pm; ☎971 724090). A second municipal tourist office (Mon–Fri 9am–8pm, Sat 9am–1.30pm; ☎971 754329) is located a few metres from the Inca train station on the northeast edge of Plaça Espanya.

out, the Cathedral was five hundred years in the making, but nevertheless, although there are architectural bits and bobs from several different eras, the church remains essentially Gothic, with massive exterior buttresses – its most distinctive feature – taking the weight off the pillars within. The whole structure derives its effect from sheer height, impressive from any angle, but startling when viewed from the waterside esplanade.

The majestic proportions of its interior are seen to best advantage from the western end, from the Portal Major (doorway). In the central nave, fourteen beautifully aligned, pencil-thin pillars rise to 21m before their ribs branch out, like fronded palm trees, to support the single-span, vaulted roof. The nave, at 44m high, is one of the tallest Gothic structures in Europe, and its 121m length is of matching grandeur. Kaleidoscopic floods of light filter in through the stained-glass windows, many of which have recently been unbricked or refurbished to their former glory.

The aisles on either side of the central nave are flanked by a long sequence of chapels, dull affairs for the most part, dominated by dusty Baroque altars of little artistic merit. The exception, and the cathedral's one outstanding example of the Baroque, is the Capella de Corpus Christi, at the head of the aisle to the left of the high altar. Just across from the chapel is a massive stone pulpit from 1531 that was moved here supposedly temporarily by the Catalan architect Antoni Gaudí when he was working on the cathedral's restoration between 1904 and 1914. The pulpit is an excellent illustration of the Plateresque style with intricate floral patterns and bustling Biblical scenes covering a clumsy structure, the upper portion of which is carried by telamons, male counterparts of the more usual caryatids.

The Museu de la Catedral

Same times and ticket as the Cathedral. The suite of three rooms that make up the enjoyable Museu de la Catedral hold an eclectic mixture of ecclesiastical treasures. The first room's most valuable exhibit, in the glass case in the middle, is a gilded silver monstrance of extraordinary delicacy, dating from the late sixteenth century. On display around the walls are assorted chalices and reliquaries and a real curiosity, the portable altar of Jaume I, a wood and silver chessboard with each square containing a bag of relics. The second room is mainly devoted to the Gothic works of the Mallorcan Primitives, a school of painters which flourished

on the island in the fourteenth and fifteenth centuries, producing strikingly naive devotional works in bold colours.

The third and final room, the Baroque chapterhouse, is entered through a playfully ornate doorway, above which a delicate Madonna is overwhelmed by lively cherubic angels. Inside, pride of place goes to the High Baroque altar surmounted by the Sacred Heart, a gory representation of the heart of Jesus that was very much in vogue during the eighteenth century. Some imagination went into the designation of the reliquaries displayed round the room: there's a piece of the flogging post, three thorns from Christ's crown, and even a piece of the gall and vinegared sponge that was offered to the crucified Jesus.

The Palau de l'Almudaina

April–Sept Mon–Fri 10am–5.45pm, Sat 10am–1.15pm; Oct–March Mon–Fri 10am–1.15pm & 4–5.15pm, Sat 10am–1.15pm; €3.20, plus €2 for audioguide; free entry on Wed to EU citizens showing their passport. Opposite the cathedral entrance stands the Palau de l'Almudaina, originally the palace of the Moorish *walis* (governors), and

PLACES Palma

▼PALAU DE L'ALMUDAINA

later of the Mallorcan kings. The present structure, built around a central courtyard, owes much of its appearance to Jaume II (1276–1311), who spent the last twelve years of his life in residence here. Jaume converted the old fortress into a lavish palace that incorporated both Gothic and Moorish features, which can be seen from the waterside esplanade below. Today the palace serves a variety of official functions, housing a series of state apartments kept in readiness for visiting dignitaries and the royal family. When the king or some other bigwig is in residence, parts of the palace are usually cordoned off; otherwise, the palace is best visited using the multilingual audioguide.

Palau March Museu

c/Palau Reial 18. April–Oct Mon–Fri 10am–6.30pm, Sat 10am–2pm; Nov–March Mon–Fri 10am–5pm, Sat 10am–2pm; €3.60; @www .fundbmarch.es. The Palau March is an extravagant affair, whose arcaded galleries, chunky columns and large stone blocks ooze power and wealth. They were erected in the 1930s in the general style of the city's earlier Renaissance mansions on behalf of the Mallorcan magnate and art collector Joan March (1880–1962), who became the wealthiest man in Franco's Spain by skilfully reinvesting the profits he made from his control of the government monopoly in tobacco – though his enemies always insisted that it was smuggling that really made him rich. Much of the palace has been turned into a museum, the highlight of which is the splendid Italianate courtyard, which is used to display a potpourri of modern art drawn from the March collection. Amongst the twenty or so pieces on display, there are two Henry Moore sculptures, a Rodin torso and a fetchingly eccentric *Orgue del Mar* (Organ of the Sea) by Xavier Corberó.

The city walls and the Parc de la Mar

A flight of steps leads down from between the cathedral and the Palau de l'Almudaina to a handsomely restored section of the Renaissance city walls, whose mighty zigzag of bastions, bridges, gates and dry moats once encased the whole city. Earlier fortifications, constructed of sandstone blocks and adobe, had depended for their efficacy on height but, by the middle of the fifteenth century, the military balance had shifted in favour of offence, with cannons now able to breach medieval city walls with comparative ease. Walls were rebuilt much lower and thicker to absorb cannon shot, while four-faced bastions – equipped with artillery platforms – projected

▼PALAU MARCH MUSEU

▲ CITY WALLS

from the line of the walls. The whole was protected by a water-filled moat with deep, sheer sides. The Habsburgs ordered work to start on the new design in the 1560s, though the chain of bastions was only completed in 1801.

From the foot of the steps below the cathedral, a wide and pleasant walkway travels along the top of the walls, providing fine views of the cathedral and an insight into the tremendous strength of the fortifications. Heading west, the walkway leads to the tiered gardens of a small Moorish-style park, which tumble down to the foot of Avinguda d'Antoni Maura, an extension of the tree-lined Passeig d'es Born (see p.63). In the opposite direction – east from the steps below the cathedral – the walkway passes above the planted palm trees, concrete terraces and ornamental lagoon of the Parc de la Mar, an imaginative and popular redevelopment of the disused land that once lay between the walls and the coastal motorway.

Wall and walkway zigzag along the south side of old Palma before fizzling out at Plaça Llorenç Villalonga. After a couple of minutes, you reach the wide stone ramp (beginning at the foot of c/Miramar) that leads down to the double Portella gateway, at the bottom of c/Portella.

▼ PORTELLA GATEWAY

▲THE BANYS ÀRABS

The Banys Àrabs

c/Can Serra 7. Daily: June–Sept 9am–8pm; Oct–May 9am–6pm; €1.50. North of the Portella gate, take the first turning right for the Banys Àrabs (Arab Baths), one of the few genuine reminders of the Moorish presence, albeit rather modest. This tenth-century brick *hammam* (bath house) consists of a small horseshoe-arched and domed chamber which was once heated through the floor. The arches rest on stone pillars, an irregular bunch thought to have been looted from the remains of the island's Roman buildings. The baths are reasonably well preserved, but if you've visited those in the Palau de l'Almudaina (see p.55), these are anticlimactic. The tables in the lush garden are good for picnics.

Casa Museu J. Torrents Lladó

c/Portella 9. Mid-Sept to mid-June Tues–Fri 10am–6pm, Sat 10am–2pm; mid-June to mid-Sept Tues–Fri 11am–7pm, Sat 10am–2pm; €3; ⓦwww .jtorrentsllado.com. The old house and studio of the Catalan artist J. Torrents Lladó (1946–1993) has been pleasantly converted into a small museum, the Casa Museu J. Torrents Lladó, celebrating his life and work. Lladó trained in Barcelona, but he rejected Modernism in the late 1960s, moving to Mallorca in 1968. He became well known as a society portraitist, painting pictures of the rich and famous in a dark and broody Baroque style, examples of which hang along with a number of landscapes, both watercolours and sticky oils.

The Museu de Mallorca

c/Portella 5. Tues–Sat 10am–7pm, Sun 10am–2pm; €2.40. The Museu de Mallorca occupies Can Aiamans, a rambling Renaissance mansion whose high-ceilinged rooms make a delightful setting for an enjoyable medley of Mallorcan artefacts, the earliest dating from prehistoric times, fleshed out by a superb assortment of Gothic paintings and some exquisite examples of *Modernista* fittings and furnishings – though note that the (multilingual) labelling is more than a tad patchy.

The collection begins in the basement, behind and to the right of the entrance, with a large and impressive section devoted to prehistoric Mallorca. There are all sorts of archeological bits and pieces here, from vases to funerary objects, and there's also an ambitious attempt to examine some of the controversies surrounding the findings. The prehistoric section leads into Roman Mallorca, whose most noteworthy relic is a battered mosaic, and then it's onto the Arab and Moorish section, which holds an exquisite selection of jewellery as well as inscribed Arab funerary tablets, and some beautiful, highly decorated wooden panelling representative of Mudéjar artistry.

Retracing your steps, cross the courtyard and climb the stairs for the first of a couple of rooms devoted to the Mallorcan Primitive painters. On display in this first room are works by the Masters of Bishop Galiana, Montesión and Castellitx and, best of the lot, a panel painting entitled *Santa Quiteria*, whose lifelike, precisely executed figures – right down to the king's wispy beard – are typical of the gifted Master of the Privileges. Beyond a room of religious statues and carved capitals, the second room of Gothic paintings is distinguished by a sequence of works by Francesc Comes (1379–1415), whose skill in catching subtle skin textures matches his Flemish contemporaries and represents a softening of the early Mallorcan Primitives' crudeness. In his striking *St George*, the saint – girl-like, with typically full lips – impales a lime-green dragon with more horns than could possibly be useful. One of the last talented exponents of the Mallorcan

Gothic, the Master of the Predellas – probably a certain Joan Rosató – is represented by his Bosch-like *Life of Santa Margalida*, each crowd of onlookers a sea of ugly, deformed faces and merciless eyes.

The ensuing rooms display the stodgy art of the Counter-Reformation, but the museum's top floor holds an engaging assortment of nineteenth- and early twentieth-century paintings by foreign artists once resident in Mallorca. Also on this floor are two room of *Modernista* fittings and furnishings, mostly retrieved from shops and houses that have since been demolished. Of particular interest are the charming wall tiles manufactured at the island's La Roqueta works. The pottery was in production for just twenty years (1897–1918), but this coincided with the vogue for the *Modernista* pieces in which La Roqueta excelled.

Can Oleza and Can Vivot

Up the hill c/Portella leads to c/Morey where, at no. 9, you'll find Can Oleza, a sixteenth-century mansion with a cool and shaded courtyard embel-

▼COURTYARD, MUSEU DE MALLORCA

lished by a handsome balustrade and a set of Ionic columns. This is one of the finest of the city's many Renaissance mansions (see box below), but like the others, it's rarely open to the public. Another excellent example is Can Vivot, an especially opulent early eighteenth-century mansion, whose spacious main courtyard, with its fetching columns and arches, is distinguished by an elegant gallery. It is located just round the back of the Església de Santa Eulalia, at c/Can Savella 4.

Església de Santa Eulalia

Plaça Santa Eulalia. Mon–Fri 7am–12.30pm & 5.45–8.30pm, Sat 7am–1pm & 4.30–8.45pm, Sun 8am–1pm & 6.30–8.30pm; free. Overshadowing the square at the top of c/Morey is the Església de Santa Eulalia, which was built on the site of a mosque in the mid-thirteenth century. It took just 25 years to complete and consequently possesses an architectural homogeneity

that's unusual for ecclesiastical Palma, though there was some later tinkering. The church is typically Gothic in construction, with a yawning nave originally designed – as in the cathedral – to give the entire congregation a view of the high altar. The bricked-up windows of today keep out most of the light and spoil the effect, but suggestions that they be cleared have always been ignored. Framing the nave, the aisles accommodate twelve shallow chapels, one of which (the first on the right) sports a delightful Gothic panel painting in finely observed Flemish style. The other chapels are standard-issue Baroque, though they pale into insignificance when compared with the hourglass-shaped high altarpiece, a flashy Baroque extravagance of colossal proportions.

This holy ground witnessed one of the more disgraceful episodes of Mallorcan history. During Easter week, 1435, a rumour went round that

Mansions in Palma

Most of medieval Palma was destroyed by fire, so the patrician **mansions** that characterize the old town today generally date from the reconstruction programme of the late seventeenth and early eighteenth centuries. Consequently they were built in the fashionable Renaissance style, with columns and capitals, loggias and arcades tucked away behind outside walls of plain stone three or four storeys high, and are surprisingly uniform in layout. Entry to almost all of these mansions was through a great arched gateway that gave onto a rectangular courtyard around which the house was built. Originally, the courtyard would have been cheered by exotic trees and flowering shrubs, and equipped with a fancy stone and ironwork well-head, where visitors could water their horses. From the courtyard, a stone exterior staircase led up to the main public rooms – with the servants' quarters below and the family's private apartments up above.

Very few of these mansions are open to the public, and all you'll see for the most part is the view from the gateway – the municipality has actually started to pay people to leave their big wooden gates open. Several have, however, passed into the public domain, the Can Aiamans, now the home of the Museu de Mallorca, being the prime example. Others worth making a detour to see are Can Oleza (p.59), Can Vivot (p.59) and Can Solleric (p.63). Only the last of these is open to the public.

Jewish townsfolk had enacted a blasphemous mock-up of the Crucifixion. There was no proof, but the Jews were promptly robbed of their possessions and condemned to be burnt at the stake unless they adopted Christianity. The ensuing mass baptism was held here at Santa Eulalia.

The Basílica de Sant Francesc

Plaça Sant Francesc. Daily 9.30am–12.30pm & 3.30–6pm, but closed Sun afternoon; €1. Occupying the site of an old Moorish soap factory, the Basílica de Sant Francesc is a domineering pile that was built for the Franciscans towards the end of the thirteenth century, though most of what you see today is seventeenth century, the result of a thoroughgoing reconstruction undertaken after the church was hit by lightning. The severe facade is pierced by a gigantic rose window of Plateresque intricacy and embellished by a Baroque doorway, the tympanum of which features a triumphant Virgin Mary engulfed by a wriggling mass of sculptured decoration. The strange statue in front of the doorway – of a Franciscan monk and a young Native American – celebrates the missionary work of Junípero Serra (see p.129), a Mallorcan priest despatched to California in 1768, who subsequently founded the cities of San Diego, Los Angeles and San Francisco.

The church is entered through its handsome Gothic cloister, but the interior is disappointingly gloomy – too dark, in fact, to pick out any but the most obvious of its features. However, you can push a switch to light the monumental high altar – it's on the right-hand side near the door to the sacristy. The altar is a gaudy Baroque affair featuring balustrades, lattice-work and clichéd figurines beneath a painted wooden statue of St George and the Dragon.

Plaça Sant Jeroni

In the depths of the old town, Plaça Sant Jeroni is a pretty little piazza set around a diminutive water fountain. The severe stone walls of a former convent, now a college, dominate one side of the square, while the Església de Sant Jeroni fills out another. The church facade is mostly a plain stone wall, but it does sport two elaborate doorways, the one to the left a swirl of carved foliage and garlands of fruit. The tympanum portrays the well-known story of Saint Jerome in the desert, during which the saint endures all sorts

▼CLOISTERS, BASÍLICA DE SANT FRANCESC

of tribulations and temptations, but still sticks true to the faith. The interior is a seventeenth-century affair with heavy stone vaulting, though unfortunately it's rarely open to the public. The highlight here is various paintings, amongst them several works by the Mallorcan Primitives, including Pere Terrencs' lively *Sant Jeroni*.

The Museu Diocesà

c/Calders 2. Mon–Fri 10am–1pm & 4–7pm; €3. With its usual home, the Bishop's Palace near the Cathedral, closed for refurbishment until at least 2005, the Museu Diocesà (Diocesan Museum) has been moved into far more modest premises, namely a mainly nineteenth-century chapel in a former seminary just off Plaça Sant Jeroni. The premises may be uninspiring, but the museum does hold an excellent collection of Mallorcan Primitives, including a charming *St Paul* panel painting by the Master of Bishop Galiana, whose crisp draughtsmanship was very much in the Catalan tradition. The painting is a didactic cartoon-strip illustrating the life of St Paul, who is shown with his Bible open and sword in hand, a militant view of the church that must have accorded well with the preoccupations of the powerful bishops of Mallorca.

A second highlight is the *Passion of Christ* by an unknown artist dubbed the Master of the Passion of Mallorca. Dated to the end of the thirteenth century, the painting follows a standard format, with a series of small vignettes outlining the story of Christ, but the detail is warm and gentle: the Palm Sunday donkey leans forward pushing his nose towards a child;

one of the disciples reaches out across the Last Supper table for the fish; and two of Jesus' disciples slip their sandals off in eager anticipation during the washing of the feet. By contrast, Alonso de Sedano's sixteenth-century *Crucifixion* is a sophisticated work of strong, deep colours within a triangulated structure. Above is the blood-spattered, pale-white body of Christ, while down below – divided by the Cross – are two groups, one of hooded mourners, the other a trio of nonchalant Roman soldiers in contemporary Spanish dress. Also noteworthy is a large and dramatic *St George and the Dragon*, a panel painting of the late fifteenth century attributed to Pere Niçard with the stern fortifications of Palma in the background.

Església de Monti-Sion

c/Monti-Sion. Usually open Mon–Fri 7–8.30am. From Plaça Sant Jeroni, c/Seminari and then c/Monti-Sion run west through one of the oldest parts of the city, a jumble of old and distinguished mansions hidden behind high stone walls. On the way, you pass the Església de Monti-Sion, whose thundering facade is a hectic heap of angels and saints, coats of arms and wriggling foliage. Below the figure of the Virgin, look out for a strangely inconclusive representation of the Devil – half-sheep, half-dragon.

Beyond the church, c/Monti-Sion leads to a crossroads: turn right along c/Pare Nadal to reach the Basílica de Sant Francesc (see p.61); alternatively, keep dead ahead and the twisting side streets will deliver you onto Plaça Santa Eulalia, a short distance from Plaça Cort.

Plaça Cort

With its elegant nineteenth-century facades, bustling Plaça Cort was named after the various legal bodies – both secular and religious – which were once concentrated here. Along with much of the rest of Spain, Mallorca possessed a truly byzantine legal system until the whole caboodle was swept away and rationalized during the Napoleonic occupation. On one side, the square is dominated by the Ajuntament (Town Hall), a debonair example of the late Renaissance style. Pop in for a look at the grand and self-assured foyer, which mostly dates from the nineteenth century, and the six folkloric *gigantones* (giant carnival figures) stored here – four in a corner, the other two tucked against the staircase.

Passeig d'es Born and Can Solleric

Distinguished by the stone sphinxes at its top and bottom, the Passeig d'es Born has been the city's principal promenade since the early fifteenth century, when the stream that ran here was diverted following a disastrous flash flood. Nowadays, this leafy avenue is too traffic-congested to be especially endearing, but it's still at the heart of the city, and close to some of Palma's most fashionable bars and restaurants. It's also overlooked by several of the city's most lavish mansions, notably the loggia of the Palau March – now the site of the *Cappuccino* café

(see p.69) – and Can Solleric (Tues–Sat 10am–2pm & 5–9pm, Sun 10am–1.30pm; free) at no. 27, a handsome Italianate structure of heavy wooden doors, marble columns and vaulted ceilings built for a family of cattle and olive - oil merchants in 1763. Recently restored, the house now displays roving exhibitions of modern art and is the temporary home of the main municipal tourist office.

Avinguda Jaume III

At the top of Passeig d'es Born, the sturdy shops and office blocks of Avinguda Jaume III, dating from the 1940s, march west towards the Passeig Mallorca. It's here you'll find some of the island's chicest clothes shops (see p.72), as well as downtown's biggest department store, El Corte Inglés (see p.72). There's something very

▼STONE SPHINX, PASSEIG D'ES BORN

engaging about the avenue – a jostle of beshorted tourists and besuited Spaniards – and the web of ancient alleys immediately to the north is another attractive corner of the city, all high stone walls and dignified old mansions focused on c/Concepció.

Plaça Mercat and Plaça Weyler

Tiny Plaça Mercat is the site of two identical *Modernista* buildings commissioned by a wealthy baker, Josep Casasayas, in 1908. Each is a masterpiece of flowing, organic lines tempered by graceful balconies and decorated with fern-leaf and butterfly motifs. Just along the street, on Plaça Weyler, stands a further *Modernista* extravagance, the magnificent Gran Hotel

of 1903. Recently scrubbed and polished, the facade boasts playful arches, balconies, columns and bay windows enlivened with intricate floral trimmings and brilliant polychrome ceramics inspired by Hispano-Arabic designs. The interior houses a café-bar, a good art bookshop and the spacious Fundació La Caixa art gallery (Tues–Sat 10am–9pm, Sun 10am–2pm; free), which organizes an excellent and wide-ranging programme of exhibitions. The permanent collection is confined to a large sample of work by the Catalan impressionist-expressionist Hermen Anglada-Camarasa, who is best known for the evocative Mallorcan land- and seascapes he produced during his sojourn on the island from 1914 to 1936.

▲ GRAN HOTEL, PLAÇA WEYLER

There's another excellent example of *Modernismo* across the street from the Gran Hotel, in the floral motifs and gaily painted wooden doorway of the Forn des Teatre (theatre bakery) at Plaça Weyler 9. A few metres away looms the Neoclassical frontage of the Teatre Principal, whose tympanum sports a fanciful relief dedicated to the nine Muses of Greek mythology. This is the city's main auditorium for classical music, ballet and opera, but at the moment it's closed for a thorough revamp.

▲MODERNISTA ARCHITECTURE

Plaça Major and Plaça Marquès del Palmer

On both sides of the Teatre Principal, steep flights of steps lead up to Plaça Major, a large pedestrianized square built on the site of the former headquarters of the Spanish Inquisition. The square, a rather formal affair with a symmetrical portico running around its perimeter, once housed the fish and vegetable market, but nowadays it's popular for its pavement cafés. On the south side of Plaça Major lies the much smaller Plaça Marquès del Palmer, a cramped setting for two fascinating *Modernista* edifices. The more dramatic is Can Rei, a five-storey apartment building splattered with polychrome ceramics and floral decoration, its centrepiece a gargoyle-like face set between a pair of winged dragons. The facade of the adjacent L'Àguila building is of similar ilk, though there's greater emphasis on window space, reflecting its original function as a department store – it's currently a shoe shop.

The Museu d'Art Espanyol Contemporani

c/Sant Miquel 11. Mon–Fri 10am–6.30pm, Sat 10.30am–2pm; free. On the pleasant shop-ping street c/Sant Miquel, the Banca March occupies a fine Renaissance mansion whose *Modernista* flourishes date from a tasteful refurbishment of 1917. The building has two entrances, one to the bank, the other to the upper-floor Museu d'Art Espanyol Contemporani, which features changing selections from the contemporary art collection of the March family (see p.56). Dozens of works by twentieth-century Spanish artists are displayed, the intention being to survey the Spanish contribution to modern art, a theme which is further developed by temporary exhibitions. The earliest piece, Picasso's *Tête de Femme* (1907), is of particular interest, being one of the first of the artist's works to be influenced by the primitive forms that were to propel him from the re-creation of natural appearances into abstract art. Miró and Dalí are also well represented, but the bulk of the collection is remorselessly modern and, although there are some touches of humour, most of it is hard to warm to, especially the allegedly "vigorous" abstractions of both the El Paso (Millares, Saura, Feito, Canogar) and the Parpalló (Sempere, Alfaro) groupings of the late 1950s.

The harbourfront – Sa Llotja

The various marinas, shipyards, fish docks, and ferry and cargo terminals that make up Palma's harbourfront extend west for several kilometres from the foot of Avinguda d'Antoni Maura. The harbour is at its prettiest at this eastern end, where a cycling and walking path skirts the sea-shore, with boats to one side and bars, restaurants, apartment blocks and the smart hotels of the Avinguda Gabriel Roca – often dubbed the Passeig Marítim – on the other. The first harbourfront landmark is the fifteenth-century Sa Llotja, the city's former stock exchange (Tues–Sat 11am–2pm & 5–9pm, Sun 11am–2pm; free). This carefully composed late-Gothic building, with four octagonal turrets, slender, spiral-ling columns and tall windows, now hosts frequent, and occa-sionally excellent, exhibitions (some of which you'll have to pay to get into). Next door, the distinguished Consolat de Mar was built in the 1660s to accom-modate the Habsburg officials who supervised maritime affairs in this part of the empire. Today, as the home of the president of the Balearic islands, it's closed to the public, but the outside is worth a second look for its pair of crusty old cannons and elegant Renaissance gallery. The forlorn-looking gate between the two buildings – the Porta Vella del Moll – originally stood at the bottom of Avinguda d'Antoni Maura, where it was the main entrance into the city from the sea, but was moved here when portions of the town wall were demolished in the 1870s.

Es Baluard

Plaça Porta de Santa Catalina s/n. Mid-June to Sept daily 10am to midnight; Oct to mid-June daily 10am–8pm; €6. The imposing bastion that once anchored the southwest corner of the city wall has been imaginatively converted into the lavish, ultramodern Es Baluard gallery of modern art. There are three floors here – two for the permanent collection, and one for temporary exhibitions – sub-divided into themed areas, from Mediterranean landscape through to the grandly named "The Sub-jectivism of the Post-Modern Era" – but perhaps the most striking feature is just how few paintings are on display. More positively, Miró, who spent a good slice of his life on Mallorca (see p.77), has a room to himself and there's a rare and unusual sample of Picasso ceramics, most memorably a striking, white, ochre and black vase-like piece entitled *Big Bird Corrida*.

Passeig Mallorca

From in front of Es Baluard, a footbridge spans the Passeig Mallorca, the walled watercourse which once served as the city moat. On the far side is a pleas-ant terraced park, whose trees, lawns, flower beds and fountains step south down towards the harbourfront, the only blot being the whopping column erected by Franco in honour – as they say – of those Balearic sailors who were loyal to the Fascist cause.

The Castell de Bellver

Oct–March Mon–Sat 8am–7pm, Sun 10am–5pm; April–Sept Mon–Fri 8am–8.30pm, Sun 10am–7pm; €1.80. Take bus #6 from Plaça de la Reina to Plaça Gomila, which leaves a steep 1km walk up the hill. If you're driving, turn off Avin-guda Joan Miró (one-way west) onto the circuitous c/Camilo José Cela. Boast-ing superb views of Palma from a wooded hilltop some 3km west of the city centre, the Castell de Bellver is a handsome, strikingly

▲CASTELL DE BELLVER

well-preserved fortress built for Jaume II at the beginning of the fourteenth century. The castle's immensely thick walls and steep ditches encircle a central keep that incorporates three imposing towers. An overhead, single-span stone arch connects the keep to a massive, freestanding tower, built as a final refuge. To enhance defence, the walls curve and bend and the interconnecting footbridges are set at oblique angles to each other. The castle was also intended to serve as a royal retreat from the summer heat, and so the austere outside walls hide a commodious, genteel-looking circular courtyard, surrounded by two tiers of inward-facing arcades that once belonged to the residential suites. Improvements in artillery, however, soon rendered the fortress obsolete, and it didn't last long as a royal residence either. As early as the 1350s the keep was in use as a prison, a function it performed until 1915. More recently, the castle interior has been turned into a museum tracking through the history of the city, with Roman statuary the main highlight. After you've explored the castle, you can wander the unsigned footpaths through the pine-scented woods that surround it.

Accommodation

Hostal Apuntadores

c/Apuntadors 8 ☎971 713491, ⊚apuntadores@ctv.es. Appealingly laid-back *hostal* in an old house on bustling c/Apuntadors. The recently renovated rooms are simple but more than adequate; all have washbasins, and some have showers. Breakfast is also available (€3–5). €35.

Hostal Brondo

c/Ca'n Brondo 1 ☎ & ☏971 719043. In a central but quiet street, this stylish little place has newly refurbished rooms with antiques and charming Rococo plasterwork. Ask for one of the rooms with a wrought-iron balcony. Shared bath €45, en suite €55.

Hostal Ritzi

c/Apuntadors 6 ☎ & ☏971 714610. Spartan rooms in an ancient but well-maintained five-storey house on one of central Palma's liveliest (and noisiest) streets. Five rooms have their own showers and two have full bathrooms; the rest have washbasins. Shared bath €35, en suite €50.

Hostal-residencia Cuba

c/Sant Magí 1 ☎971 738159, ☏971 403131. Twenty attractive, well-appointed rooms (all en suite) in a beautifully restored *Modernista* stone house of 1904, with a pretty little tower and balustrade and a rooftop sun terrace. Overlooks the harbour and the bottom of busy Avgda Argentina. Two rooms have a/c at no extra cost. €35.

Hotel Convent de la Missió

c/Missió 7A. ⊕ 971 227347, ⊛ www .conventdelamissio.com. Owned by two architects, this stunning new hotel is decorated in ultra-minimalist style, with big white spaces punctuated with strategically placed works of art. The elegant restaurant (evenings only) is an additional bonus. €160.

Hotel Dalt Murada

c/Almudaina 6 ⊕ 971 425300, ⊛ www .daltmurada.com. This magnificent sixteenth-century mansion has kept much of its original architecture and decoration, but without compromising on comforts and conveniences. Many rooms have wonderful rooftop views of the old city, and some also have terraces. Breakfast is served in the garden on fine days. Breakfast included. €130.

Hotel Saratoga

Passeig Mallorca 6 ⊕ 971 727240, ⊛ www.hotelsaratoga.es. Bright, modern, centrally located hotel in a smart seven-storey block complete with a rooftop café and swimming pool. Rooms are neat and trim, with marble floors and balconies either overlooking the boulevard or an interior courtyard and pool. Breakfast included. €140.

Hotel Sol Jaime III

Passeig Mallorca 14 ⊕ 971 725943, ⊕ 971 725946. Agreeable three-star with smart modern rooms, most with balconies. Front rooms overlook the handsome Passeig Mallorca, and chic shopping is just around the corner. Decor consists of art prints and marble touches. €100.

Hotel-residencia Born

c/Sant Jaume 3 ⊕ 971 712942, ⊛ www.hotelborn.com. Delightful hotel in an excellent downtown location, set in a refurbished mansion with a lovely courtyard where you can have breakfast under the palm trees. The rooms, most of which face onto the courtyard, are comfortable if a little care-worn, and have a/c, though not all have private bathrooms. It's a popular spot, so book early in high season. Breakfast included. €70.

Hotel-residencia Palacio Ca Sa Galesa

c/Miramar 8 ⊕ 971 715400, ⊛ www .palaciocasagalesa.com. Charmingly renovated seventeenth-century mansion set amongst the narrow alleys of the oldest part of town, with just twelve luxurious and tastefully furnished rooms and suites. There's also an indoor heated swimming pool (set in a renovated Roman bath) and fine views of the city from the roof terrace. Opened in the 1980s, this was one of the first deluxe hotels to occupy an old island mansion and its success set something of a trend. €220.

Cafés and tapas bars

Bar Bosch

Plaça Rei Joan Carles I. Daily 8am–2am. One of the most popular and inexpensive *tapas* bars in town, the traditional haunt of the city's intellectuals and usually humming with conversation. At peak times you'll need to be assertive to get served.

Bon Lloc

c/Sant Feliu 7. Mon–Sat 1–4pm. One of the few vegetarian café-restaurants on the island, with good food at low prices in an informal, homely atmosphere. No menu as such, but a selection of dishes with a set price of around €12. Very popular.

La Bóveda

Passeig Sagrera 3. Daily 1.30–4pm & 8.30pm–12.30am. One of the city's best *tapas* bars, this smart and busy spot offers air-conditioned eating inside as well as an outside terrace. Authentic *Mallorquín* and Spanish *tapas* start from as little as €4. Not to be confused with its sister, the *Taberna La Bóveda* – see p.72.

see p.72

▼ LA BÓVEDA

▲ CA'N JOAN DE S'AIGO

Ca'n Joan de S'Aigo

c/Can Sanç 10. Daily except Tues 8am–9pm. A long-established coffee house with wonderful, freshly baked *ensaimadas* (spiral pastry buns) and fruit-flavoured mousses to die for. Charming decor too, from the kitsch water fountain to the traditional Mallorcan green-tinted chandeliers. It's on a tiny alley near Plaça Santa Eulalia – take c/Sant Crist and its continuation c/Canisseria, then turn right. There's another more modern, but decoratively similar branch at c/Baró Santa Maria del Sepulcre 5, off Avgda Jaume III (same hours).

Cappuccino

c/Conquistador s/n, Palau March. Daily 8am to midnight, sometimes later. Attractive terrace café in a great setting on the patio of the Palau March, overlooking the Passeig d'es Born. Offers an interesting selection of salads and sandwiches, as does its sister outlet, located in a handsome old mansion at c/Sant Miquel 53 (similar hours).

La Cueva

c/Apuntadors 5. Mon–Sat noon–midnight, sometimes later. Small and busy *tapas* bar, one of several on this street, with a rack of liquors behind the bar and hocks of meat hanging up in front. Reasonable prices and tasty food, including grilled prawns and other seafood.

Lizarran

c/Ca'n Brondo 6. Daily 1.30–4pm & 9pm–midnight. Delightful and popular little place dishing up Basque-style *tapas* – such as smoked salmon with chopped onions, and artichoke hearts with pepper and bacon, all served on a small slice of French bread.

El Pesquero (also known as Café Port Pesquer)

Avgda Gabriel Roca s/n. Daily from 10am till late. Bright and breezy café on the harbourfront a few minutes' walk west of Avgda d'Antoni Maura, overlooking the jetty where the fishing boats come in. The open-air terrace bar is a good spot to soak up the evening sun, and there's an excellent *menú del día* (Mon–Fri; €12.50).

El Pilon

c/Cifre 4. Mon–Sat from 1pm till late. Vibrant, cramped and crowded *tapas* bar on a sidestreet off the north end of Passeig d'es Born, serving all manner of Spanish and Mallorcan dishes at very reasonable prices. Bags of atmosphere.

La Taberna del Caracol

c/Sant Alonso 2. Mon–Sat 1–3.30pm & 8–11.30pm. Delicious *tapas* and fabulous desserts in a handsome

▲EL PILON

Renaissance mansion deep in the depths of the old town. *Tapas* in the day and dinner at night.

Restaurants

Aramís

c/Montenegro 1 ☎971 725232. Mon–Fri 1–3pm & 8–11pm, Sat 8–11pm. Set in an old stone mansion, though the decor is resolutely minimalist, this excellent restaurant has an imaginative menu with an international slant – pumpkin ravioli, wild mushrooms en croute – and there's an unbeatable *menú del día* (€12.50) plus wonderful house red. Reservations advised.

Asador Tierra Aranda

c/Concepció 4, off Avgda Jaume III ☎971 714256. Tues–Sat 1–3pm & 8–11pm. A long-established and fairly formal carnivore's paradise in an old mansion: meats either grilled over open fires or roasted in wood-fired ovens, with suckling pig and lamb a speciality. You can also eat in the very pleasant garden. Reservations advised.

Caballito del Mar

Passeig Sagrera 5 ☎971 721074. Tues–Sun 1–4pm & 8–11.30pm. Across the plaza from Sa Llotja, this infinitely agreeable restaurant, with smart tablecloths and fast-moving waiters, offers an extensive range of fish. The *daurada amb sal al forn* (sea bream baked in salt) is a house speciality. Main courses hover around €20. Reservations essential in summer.

Ca'n Carlos

c/Aigua 5 ☎971 713869. Mon–Sat 1–4pm & 8–11pm. Charming, family-run restaurant featuring exquisite Mallorcan cuisine that takes in dishes such as cuttlefish and snails. The menu isn't extensive, but everything is beautifully and imaginatively prepared and there's a daily special as well as a fish of the day. Main courses range from €13 to €31.

Es Parlament

c/Conquistador 11 ☎971 726026. Mon–Sat 1–4pm & 8–11pm. All gilt-wood mirrors and chandeliers, this old and polished restaurant specializes in paella. The tasty and reasonably priced *menú del día* is recommended, too. A favourite hangout of local politicians and lawyers. Dinner reservations advised.

Flor de Loto

c/Vallseca 7 ☎971 717778. Tues–Sun 7pm–1am. Specializing in vegetarian and fish dishes, including risottos and curries (€9–13), this delightful new place has a relaxing atmosphere enhanced by discreet world music and the occasional live guitarist. Try the cold yoghurt soup with tiny grilled shrimps (€6).

Forn de Sant Joan

c/Sant Joan 4 ☎971 728422. Daily 7pm–midnight. Set in an old bakery, this smart and extremely popular family-run Catalan restaurant does a range of fine fish dishes (€15–20) and *tapas* (from €6) – try the red peppers stuffed with shellfish, followed by the lemon and cinnamon mousse.

Mangiafuoco

Plaça Vapor 4, Santa Catalina ☎971 451072. Daily except Tues 1.30–3.30pm & 8–11.30pm. Tuscan-owned restaurant-cum-wine bar offering top-notch Italian food and specializing in dishes featuring truffles, which are flown in weekly from Tuscany. Prepare to be wowed by the *pappardelle al tartuffo*, especially when washed down with one of the superb house wines. Santa Catalina is an almost fashionable suburb, about fifteen to twenty minutes' walk west of the Cathedral.

Bars

Abaco

Just off c/Apuntadors at c/Sant Joan 1 ☎971 714939. Daily 9pm–2am. Set in a charming Renaissance mansion, this is easily Palma's most unusual bar, with an interior straight out of a Busby Berkeley musical: fruits cascading down its stairway, caged birds hidden amid patio foliage and elegant music playing in the background. Drinks are extremely expensive (cocktails cost as much as €15), but you're never hurried into buying one. It is, however, too sedate to be much fun if you're on the razzle.

Barcelona Jazz Café Club

c/Apuntadors 5. Mon–Thurs 8.30pm–1am, Fri & Sat 8.30pm–3am. Groovy little spot on one of the busiest streets in town, with jazz, blues and Latin sounds.

Pacha

Avgda Gabriel Roca 42 ☎971 455 908. Loud, popular and raucous housey disco with a dancefloor and a couple of bars inside and another bar outside in the garden. A 20min walk west of the town centre along the harbourfront. There's a gay night, "Pacha Loca", at least once a week, usually Sun. Entrance (usually) €15.

Taberna La Bóveda

c/Boteria 3, off Plaça Llotja. Daily 1.30–4pm & 8.30pm–12.30am. Classy, fashionable bar with long, wide windows and wine stacked high along the back wall – come

early or prepared to get in. Also see *La Bóveda* above.

Tito's

Plaça Gomila 3 ☎971 730 017. With its stainless-steel and glass exterior, this long-established nightspot looks like something from a sci-fi film. Outdoor lifts carry you up from Avgda Gabriel Roca (the back entrance) to the dance floor, which pulls in huge international crowds – or you can go in through the front entrance on Plaça Gomila. The music (anything from house to mainstream pop) lacks conviction, but it's certainly loud. Admission €18.

Shopping

Camper

Avgda Jaume III 16 & Sant Miquel 17. Mon–Sat 10am–8.30pm. Love them or hate them, Camper shoes are extraordinarily popular and they are made in Mallorca. This outlet sells the range.

Casa del Mapa

c/Sant Domingo 11. Mon–Fri 10am–1.30pm & 5–7.30pm, Sat 10am–1pm. Good driving and walking maps of Mallorca can be surprisingly hard to get hold of, but this specialist map shop – the only one on the island – rectifies matters.

Casa del Olivo

c/Pescateria Vella, a tiny alley off c/Jaume II. Mon–Fri 10.30am–1.30pm & 4.30–8pm. Old-fashioned place selling a veritable Aladdin's cave of olive-wood carvings, with everything from spoons, bread boards and salad bowls through to more eccentric-looking items of no discernible (surely not decorative) purpose.

▼LA CASA DEL OLIVO

Palma **PLACES**

Colmado Santo Domingo

c/Sant Domingo 1. Mon–Fri
10am–1.30pm & 5–7.30pm, Sat
10am–1pm. A tiny shop engulfed
with hanging sausages of every
description, not to mention
fresh fruit and veg. There's a
very similar shop, Colmado
Colom, but more of a deli,
less of a sausagery, a few paces
further down the street.

El Corte Inglés

Avgda Jaume III 15. Mon–Sat
9.30am–9.30pm. The biggest and
best department store in the city
centre, which – as you might
expect – sells just about everything. Has a substantial food and
drink section in its basement,
where you can track down lots
of Mallorcan wines.

Forn Fondo

c/Unió 15. Mon–Sat 7.45am–8.30pm &
Sun 7.45am–2pm. Palma has lots of
good cake and pastry shops (*pas-
telerías*) and this is one of the best.
An excellent second option is
Forn des Teatre, just along the
street at Plaça Weyler 9 (Mon–Sat
9am–12.30pm & 4.30–7.30pm).

La Bodeguilla

c/Sant Jaume 3. Daily 11am–11.30pm.
In a glossily refurbished, warren-
like town house off Avgda
Jaume III, this establishment has
a restaurant upstairs and a wine
bar-cum-wine merchants down
below. Drink in or take home
– from their excellent range
of wines, including all the best
Mallorcan vintages, with Binissalem reds leading the way.

Majorica

Avgda Jaume III 11. Mon–Fri
9.30am–1.30pm & 4.30–8pm, Sat
9.30am–1.30pm. The official
outlet for the main manufac-
turer of Mallorca's well-known
artificial pearls. Made from glass
globules painted with many
layers of a glutinous liquid
primarily composed of fish
scales, the industry is based in
Manacor, in the heart of the
island.

Vidrias Gordiola

c/Victòria 2. Mon–Fri 10am–1.30pm &
4.30–8pm, Sat 10am–1.30pm. Glass-
making is a traditional island
craft and this shop, an outlet for
the main Mallorcan manufac-
turer, has a fine range of clear
and tinted glassware, from bowls,
vases and lanterns through to
some wonderfully intricate
chandeliers.

The Bay of Palma

Arched around the sheltered waters of the Bay of Palma (Badia de Palma) are the package-tourist resorts of sun, sex and booze folklore. This thirty-kilometre-long stretch of coastline is divided into a score or more resorts and, although it's often difficult to fathom where one ends and another begins, each has evolved its own identity, either in terms of the nationalities they attract, the income group they appeal to, or the age range they cater for.

East of Palma lies S'Arenal, mainly geared up for young Germans, with dozens of pounding bars and all-night clubs as well as one of Mallorca's best beaches, the Platja de Palma. West of Palma, the coast bubbles up into the low, rocky hills and sharp coves that prefigure the mountains further west. The sandy beaches here are far smaller but the terrain makes the tourist development seem less oppressive. Cala Major, the first stop, was once the playground of the super rich. It's hit grittier times, but some of the grand old buildings have survived and the Fundació Pilar i Joan Miró makes a fascinating detour. The neighbouring resort of Illetes is a good deal more polished, boasting comfortable hotels and attractive cove beaches, while, moving west again, Portals Nous has an affluent and exclusive marina. Next comes British-dominated Palma Nova, a major package-holiday destination popular with all ages, and adjacent Magaluf, where high-rise hotels, thumping nightlife and a substantial sandy beach cater to a youthful and very British crowd. South of Magaluf, the charming cove beach of Portals Vells is a real surprise, sheltered by an undeveloped, pine-studded peninsula. West of Magaluf, the coastal highway leaves the Badia de Palma for unpretentious Santa Ponça before pushing on to Peguera, a large, sprawling family resort with attractive sandy beaches. Next door – and much more endearing – is tiny

Getting around

Public **transport** along the Bay of Palma is fast and efficient, with most bus services starting from Palma's Plaça Espanya. **EMT** bus #15 travels the old coastal road east through Ca'n Pastilla to S'Arenal, their bus #20 heads west as far as Palma Nova and Calvià, and bus #3 runs to Cala Major. In addition, the **Transabús** company operates the "Playasol" routes, with frequent buses from Plaça Espanya, Plaça Rei Joan Carles I and other Palma city centre points, west to Illetes, Magaluf, Santa Ponça, Peguera and Camp de Mar. For further details, ring **tib** (☎971 17 7777).

Driving is straightforward: the *autopista* shoots along the coast from S'Arenal right round to Palma Nova and then slices across a narrow peninsula to reach Santa Ponça and Peguera. Alternatively, you can take the much slower old coastal road (numbered the C719 west of Palma), which meanders through most of the resorts.

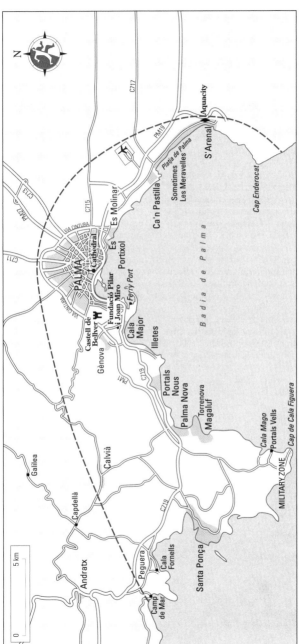

Cala Fornells, where pretty villas thread along the coastal hills. From here, it's another short hop to the pleasant bay which encloses the burgeoning resort of Camp de Mar.

The Platja de Palma

The **Platja de Palma**, the four-kilometre stretch of sandy beach that defines the four coterminous (and indistinguishable) resorts of Ca'n Pastilla, Sometimes, Les Meravelles and S'Arenal, is crowded with serious sun-seekers, a sweating throng of bronzed and oiled bodies slowly roasting in the heat. The beach is also a busy pick-up place, the spot for a touch of verbal foreplay before the night-time bingeing begins. It is, as they say, fine if you like that sort of thing – though older visitors look rather marooned. A wide and pleasant walkway lined with palm trees runs behind the beach and this, in turn, is edged by a long

sequence of bars, restaurants and souvenir shops. A toy-town tourist "train" shuttles up and down the walkway, but there's so little to distinguish one part of the beach from another that it's easy to become disoriented. To maintain your bearings, keep an eye out for the series of smart, stainless-steel beach bars, each numbered and labelled, in Castilian, *balneario*, strung along the shore: *Balneario* no. 15 is by the Ca'n Pastilla marina, while no. 1 is near S'Arenal harbour.

Singling out any part of this massive complex is a pretty pointless exercise, but the area around S'Arenal harbour does at least have a concentration of facilities. There's car rental, currency exchange, boat trips and nightclubs as well as a couple of above-average places to eat.

Aquacity

Palma–S'Arenal road, km 15. July–Aug daily 10am–6pm; May–June & Sept–Oct daily 10am–5pm; €19.50; ☎971 440000. Between the *autopista* and the eastern edge of the resort, about 15km east of Palma lies Aquacity, a huge leisure complex of swimming pools, water flumes and kiddies' playgrounds.

Cala Major

Crowded **Cala Major** snakes along a hilly stretch of coastline a kilometre or two to the west of Palma's ferry port. Overlooking the main street (which comprises a section of the C719 coast road), occasional *Modernista* mansions and the luxurious *Nixe* hotel are reminders of halcyon days when the resort was a byword for elegance. The king of Spain still runs a palace here – the Palacio de Marivent, on the main street close to the *autopista* at the east end of the resort.

▼PLATJA DE PALMA

▲FUNDACIÓ PILAR I JOAN MIRÓ

The Fundació Pilar i Joan Miró

c/Joan de Saridakis 29, Cala Major. Mid-May to mid-Sept Tues–Sat 10am–7pm, Sun 10am–3pm; mid-Sept to mid-May Tues–Sat 10am–6pm, Sun 10am–3pm; ✪ www.a–palma.es /fpjmiro; €4.80.Opposite the Palacio de Marivent in Cala Major, the signposted turning to Gènova leads up the hill for 500m to the Fundació Pilar i Joan Miró, where the painter Joan Miró lived and worked for much of the 1950s, 1960s and 1970s. Initially – from 1920 – the young Miró was involved with the Surrealists in Paris and contributed to all their major exhibitions: his wild squiggles, supercharged with bright colours, prompted André Breton, the leading theorist of the movement, to describe Miró as "the most Surrealist of us all". In the 1930s he adopted a simpler style, abandoning the decorative complexity of his earlier work for a more mini-malist use of symbols, though the highly coloured forms remained. Miró returned to Barcelona, the city of his birth, in 1940, where he continued

to work in the Surrealist tra-dition, though as an avowed opponent of Franco his position was uneasy. In 1957 he moved to Mallorca, its relative isola-tion offering a degree of safety. His wife and mother were both Mallorcan, which must have influenced his decision, as did the chance to work in his own purpose-built studio with its view of the coast. Even from the relative isolation of Franco's Spain he remained an influential figure, prepared to experiment with all kinds of media, right up until his death here in Cala Major in 1983.

The expansive hillside prem-ises of the Fundació include Miró's old studio, an unassum-ing affair with views over the bay that has been left pretty much as it was at the time of his death. It's worth a quick gander for a flavour of how the man worked – tackling a dozen or so canvases at the same time – but unfortunately you're only allowed to peer through the windows. Opposite are the angular lines of the bright-white art gallery, the Edificio Estrella, which displays a rotating and representative sample of the artist's prolific work. Miró was nothing if not productive, and the Fundació holds 134 paintings, 300 engravings and 105 drawings, as well as sculptures, gouaches and preliminary sketches – more than six thousand works in all. There are no guarantees as to what will be on display, but you're likely to see a decent selection of his paintings, the familiar dream-like squiggles and half-recognizable shapes that are intended to conjure up the unconscious, with free play often given to erotic associations. The gallery also stores a comprehensive collection of Miró documents and occasionally hosts exhibitions.

Illetes and Platja Cala Comtesa

Well-heeled Illetes (sometimes written Illetas), just along the coast from Cala Major and 7km west of Palma, comprises a ribbon of restaurants, hotels and apartment buildings which bestride the steep hills that rise high above the rocky shoreline. There's precious little space left, but at least the generally low-rise buildings are of manageable proportions. A string of tiny cove beaches punctuates the coast, the most attractive being the pine-shaded Platja Cala Comtesa, at the southern end of the resort, alongside a military zone.

Portals Nous

To the west of Illetes lies the larger resort of Portals Nous, a ritzy settlement where polished mansions fill out the green and hilly terrain abutting the coast. There's a tiny beach too, set beneath the cliffs and reached via a flight of steps at the foot of c/Passatge del Mar. The drawback is the main drag (also the C719), which is disappointingly drab, but it does lead to the glitzy marina, one of Mallorca's most exclusive, where the boats look more like ocean liners than pleasure yachts – it's a favoured hang-out for the king and his cronies.

Palma Nova

Old Mallorca hands claim that Palma Nova, 4km west of Portals Nous, was once a beauty spot, and certainly its wide and shallow bay, with good beaches among a string of bumpy headlands, still has its moments. But for the most part, the bay has been engulfed by a broad, congested sweep of hotels and tourist facilities. With the development comes a vigorous nightlife and a plethora of accommodation options on or near the seashore – though, as elsewhere, most are block-booked by tour operators throughout the season.

▼PORTALS NOUS MARINA

Calvià

Some 6km north of Palma Nova, tucked away in the hills behind the coast, is the tiny town of Calvià, the region's administrative centre – hence the oversized town hall, paid for by the profits of the tourist industry. Dating from 1245, the parish church of Sant Joan Baptista (daily 10am–1pm) dominates the town, though the building's Gothic subtleties mostly disappeared during a nineteenth-century refurbishment that left a crude bas-relief carving of the Garden of Gethsemane above the main door. There are pleasant views across the surrounding countryside from the church and the adjacent square holds a modern mural depicting the island's history. Opposite the square, *Bar Bauza* serves bocadillos, coffee and pastries, either inside or outside in the pretty little courtyard.

From Calvià, it's a short drive west to Capdellà and the Serra de Tramuntana mountains, covered in Chapter 3, starting on p.84.

Magaluf

Torrenova, on the chunky headland at the far end of Palma Nova, is a cramped and untidy development that slides into Magaluf, whose high-rise towers march across the next bay down the coast. For years a bargain-basement package-holiday destination, Magaluf finally lost patience with its youthful British visitors in 1996. The local authorities won a court order allowing them to demolish twenty downmarket hotels in an attempt to end – or at least control – the annual binge of "violence, drunkenness and open-air sex" that, they argued,

▲BRITISH PUB, MAGALUF

characterized the resort. The high-rise hotels were duly dynamited and an extensive clean-up programme subsequently freshened up the resort's appearance. However, short of demolishing the whole lot, there's not too much anyone can do with the deadening concrete of the modern town centre – and the demolished blocks will anyway be replaced, albeit by more upmarket hotels. These draconian measures have brought some improvement, but the resort's British visitors remain steadfastly determined to create, or at least patronize, a bizarre caricature of their homeland: it's all here, from beans-on-toast with Marmite to lukewarm pints of lager.

Aquapark and Western Water Park

May–Oct daily 10am–5/6pm; €17; ☎971 131371. Stuck on the western edge of Magaluf, Aquapark is a giant-sized water park with swimming pools, water chutes and flumes which rivals S'Arenal's Aquacity. Across the road is a second theme park,

Western Water Park (May–Oct daily 10am–5/6pm; €15.50; ☎971 131203). The main event here is a replica Wild West town – one of the most incongruous sights around – as well as a water park.

Cap de Cala Figuera

In contrast to most of the rest of the coast, the eastern reaches of the Cap de Cala Figuera, the pine-clad peninsula that extends south of Magaluf, have been barely touched by the developers, though the downside is that there is no public transport beyond the resort, so you either have to drive, walk or cycle. The clearly signposted road south onto the peninsula begins on the west side of Magaluf, where the *autopista* merges into the C719. After about 1.5km, the road cuts past the Aquapark theme park (see above) and then keeps

▼PORTALS VELLS BEACH

straight at a fork where the road to Santa Ponça (see below) curves off to the right. South of the fork, the road narrows into a country lane, passing a golf course before heading off into the woods. After about 4km, a steep, kilometre-long turning on the left leads down to Cala Mago (still signposted in Castilian as Playa El Mago), where a rocky little headland with a shattered guard house has lovely beaches to either side. Park and walk down to whichever cove takes your fancy: the nudist beach on the right with its smart café-restaurant, or the delightful pine-shaded strand on the left with its beach bar, tiny port and sprinkling of villas. Both provide sunbeds and showers.

Continuing a further 600m past the Cala Mago turning, a second side road cuts for a kilometre down to the cove beach of Portals Vells. Despite a bar-restaurant and a handful of villas, it remains a pleasant, pine-scented spot of glistening sand, rocky cliffs and clear blue water, especially appealing early in the morning before it gets crowded. Clearly visible from the beach are the caves of the headland on the south side of the cove. A footpath leads to the most interesting, an old cave church where the holy-water stoup and altar have been cut out of the solid rock – the work of shipwrecked Genoese seamen, according to local legend.

Beyond the Portals Vells turning, the road continues south for 1.5km as far as a broken-down barbed-wire fence at the start of a disused military zone. You can't drive any further and you're not supposed to walk beyond the fence either, but some people do, braving the no-entry signs to scramble through

▲ CALA FORNELLS

the pine woods and out along the headland for about 1.5km to reach the solitary Cap de Cala Figuera lighthouse.

Santa Ponça

West of Magaluf, the C719 trims the outskirts of Santa Ponça, one of the less endearing of the resorts that punctuate this stretch of coast. Mostly a product of the 1980s, it's a sprawling conurbation where the concrete high-rises of yesteryear have been abandoned for a pseudo-vernacular architecture that's littered the hills with scores of suburbanite villas. That said, the setting is magnificent, with rolling green hills flanking a broad bay, whose spacious white sandy beaches offer safe bathing.

If you want to go diving, Zoea Mallorca, at the Club Náutico Santa Ponça, Via de la Cruz s/n (☎971 691444, ⓦwww .zoeamallorca.com) organizes dives and courses for all levels.

Peguera

Sprawling Peguera, about 6km from Santa Ponça, is strung out along a lengthy, partly pedestrianized main street – the Avinguda de Peguera – immediately behind several generous sandy beaches. There's nothing remarkable about the place, but it does have an easy-going air

and is a favourite with families and older visitors. The C719 loops right round Peguera and the easiest approach, if you're just after the beach, is from the west: head into the resort along the main street and park anywhere you can before you reach the pedestrianized part of the Avinguda de Peguera, where the town's baffling one-way system sends you weaving through the resort's side streets.

Cala Fornells

Two signed turnings on the west side of Peguera lead over to the neighbouring (and much prettier) resort of Cala Fornells. The first, more westerly turning is on the edge of Peguera, the second is at the Casa Pepe supermarket. Take the second turning and the road climbs up to a string of chic, *pueblo*-style houses that perch on the sea cliffs, which trail round to the tiny centre of the resort, where a wooded cove is set around a minuscule beach – and concreted sunbathing slabs. Cala Fornells does tend to get overcrowded during the daytime, but at night the peace and quiet returns, which makes it a good base for a holiday, especially as it possesses a couple of particularly appealing hotels. You can also stroll out into the surrounding woods along a wide, dirt track which runs up behind the hotels, cutting across the pine-scented hills towards the stony cove beach of Caló d'es Monjo, 1.5km to the west.

Camp de Mar

Tucked away among the hills 3km west of Peguera, Camp de Mar has an expansive beach and fine bathing, though the scene is marred by the presence of two thumping great hotels dropped right on the seashore – the *Hotel Playa*, a British favourite, and the smarter, four-star *Club Camp de Mar*, which caters mainly to Germans. Both are modern high-rises equipped with spacious, balconied bedrooms, and both can be booked only through packaging agents. The resort is also in the middle of a massive expansion, with brand-new villa complexes now trailing back from the beach in an all-too-familiar semi-suburban sprawl. All the same, the

▼CAMP DE MAR

beach is an amiable spot to soak up the sun, and it's hard to resist the eccentric café stuck out in the bay and approached via a rickety walkway on stilts.

A minor road twists west from Camp de Mar over wooded hills to Port d'Andratx (see p.101).

Accommodation

Hotel Bon Sol

Passeig d'Illetes 30, Illetes ☎971 402111, ⊛www.ila-chateau.com /bon_sol. Appealing, family-run hotel with pseudo-Moorish architectural flourishes that tumbles down the cliffs to the seashore – and its own artificial beach. It has all the conveniences you would expect from a four-star hotel, but the beach pool, surrounded by dense greenery, is especially appealing. The better rooms have fine views out over the bay. Its clientele is staid and steady, befitting the antique-crammed interior. About 8km from downtown Palma. Closed late Nov to late Dec. €170.

Hotel Cala Fornells

Platja Cala Fornells s/n, Cala Fornells ☎971 686950, ⊛www.calafornells .com. Spick and span four-star hotel in a modern green-shuttered block overlooking the concrete sunbathing slabs of the resort's tiny beach. Ninety rooms, each neatly presented. Closed Nov & Dec. €160.

Hotel Coronado

Platja Cala Fornells s/n, Cala Fornells ☎971 686800, ⊛www.hotelcoronado .com. Spruce, modern hotel block, where most of the 140 bedrooms have sea views and balconies. Smashing location above Cala Fornells cove-beach. Closed Nov & Dec. €170.

Hotel Nixe Palace

Avgda Joan Miró, Cala Major 269 ☎971 700888, ☎971 403171. Once the haunt of the super-rich, the resort of Cala Major, about 5km west of downtown Palma, hit the skids until efforts were made to revamp the place in the 1990s. The prime example of the refit was the refurbishment of this hotel, a luxurious block with Art Deco references that backs onto the ocean. Five-star hotel with all mod cons, including 24hr room service and swimming pools. €260.

Hotel Portixol

c/Sirena 27, Es Portixol ☎971 271800, ⒲www.portixol.com. Es Portixol, just a couple of kilometres east of Palma cathedral, was once the preserve of the city's fishermen, who docked their boats at either of its sheltered coves – one is now a marina, the other is used by locals for sports and bathing. Es Portixol slipped into the doldrums in the 1960s, but it's now on the up, the trendsetter being this splendid Swedish-owned hotel, a very urban and urbane spot with all sorts of finessed details, from creative backlighting through to guest room TV cabinets that look like mini-beach cabins. It's all good fun but note that it's worth paying extra for a room with a sea view. There's an outside swimming pool and an excellent restaurant, where you can dine either in or outside looking out at the ocean. €150.

Restaurants

Flanigan's

Portals Nous harbour ☎971 676117. One of the best – some would say *the* best – restaurant in Portals Nous. Nautical decor and international fusion cuisine with the emphasis on seafood. Seating is either in plush rooms inside or on the marina-facing terrace. Main courses from €20.

La Gran Tortuga

Aldea Cala Fornells 1, Peguera ☎971 685023. Lunch & dinner; closed Mon. This is the best restaurant in town, overlooking the seashore on the road from the Casa Pepe supermarket to Cala Fornells. It serves super seafood, has a terrace bar and even boasts its own swimming pool. A three-course evening meal will set you back about €35, but you can enjoy its excellent lunches for much less.

Méson Ca'n Torrat

c/Major 29, Calvià ☎971 670682. Dinner only; closed Tues. Appealing little restaurant just down the hill from the church of Sant Joan Baptista. Specializes in roast leg of lamb and suckling pig. Moderate prices with main courses from around €17.

Tristan

Portals Nous harbour ☎971 675547. Lunch & dinner; closed Mon. Nouvelle cuisine at this deluxe harbourside restaurant with two Michelin stars. Count on around €100 per person for dinner. Reservations essential.

Shopping

Fundació Pilar i Joan Miró

c/Joan de Saridakis 29, Cala Major. Mid-May to mid-Sept Tues–Sat 10am–7pm, Sun 10am–3pm; mid-Sept to mid-May Tues–Sat 10am–6pm, Sun 10am–3pm; ⒲www.a–palma.es/fpjmiro. Excellent museum shop selling everything from T-shirts, toys and ceramics to contemporary art books with the emphasis on the vast oeuvre of Joan Miró. For a description of the museum itself, see p.77.

Western Mallorca

Mallorca is at its scenic best in the gnarled ridge of the Serra de Tramuntana, the imposing mountain range which stretches the length of the northwest shore, with rearing peaks and plunging seacliffs intermittently punctuated by valleys of olive and citrus groves. Midway along is Sóller, an antiquated merchants' town that serves as a charming introduction to the region, especially when reached on the scenic train line from Palma. From Sóller, it's a short hop down to the coast to Port de Sóller, a popular resort on a deep and expansive bay,

while the nearby mountain valleys shelter the bucolic stone-built villages of Fornalutx, Orient and Alaró, as well as the oasis-like gardens of the Jardins d'Alfàbia.

Alaró is also close to Binissalem, one of the most diverting little towns of the island's central plain, Es Pla. Southwest of Sóller, the principal coastal road, the C710, threads up through the mountains to reach the beguiling village of Deià and then Son Marroig, the mansion of the Habsburg archduke, Ludwig Salvator. Beyond lies

the magnificent Carthusian monastery of Valldemossa, whose echoing cloisters briefly accommodated George Sand and Frédéric Chopin during the 1830s. From here, it's another short haul to the gracious *hacienda* of La Granja, and the picturesque mountain hamlets of Banyalbufar and Estellencs. Leaving the coast

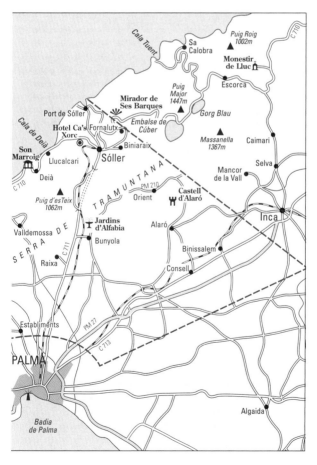

Trains, trams and buses

The 28-kilometre train journey from Palma to Sóller (☎902 364711, ☎www .trendesoller.com) is a delight, dipping and cutting through the mountains and fertile valleys of the Serra de Tramuntana. The line was completed in 1911 to transport oranges and lemons to Palma, at a time when it took a full day to make the trip by road. The rolling stock is tremendously atmospheric, with narrow carriages – the gauge is only 914mm – that look like they've come out of an Agatha Christie novel. There are six departures daily from Palma station throughout the year and the ride takes just under an hour and a quarter. A one-way ticket costs €6.50, €11 return. Trains from Palma link with the vintage trams that clunk down from Sóller to the coast at Port de Sóller, 5km away. Trams depart every half-hour or hour daily from 7am to 8pm and the fifteen-minute journey costs €2 each way.

There's a fast and frequent bus service from Palma to Sóller and Port de Sóller along the C711 road, which tunnels straight through the mountains as it approaches the coast. Another frequent bus links Palma with Sóller via Valldemossa, Son Marroig and Deià, and a further service runs along the C710 from Andratx to Sóller five times a week. For bus timetable enquiries, call ☎971 177777.

behind, you drift inland out of the mountains and into the foothills that precede the market town of Andratx, a crossroads town with easy access to the tiny resort of Sant Elm and the larger harbour-cum-resort of Port d'Andratx. Most of the region's coastal villages have

a tiny, shingle strip – nothing more. The twin beaches of Port de Sóller possess the longest strips of sand hereabouts, but the sand-less coves at Deià and Estellencs are much more appealing for their wild and wonderful setting.

Sóller

Sóller is one of the most laid-back and enjoyable towns on Mallorca, as well as being an ideal base for exploring the surrounding mountains. Rather than any specific sight, it's the general flavour of the place that appeals, with the town's narrow, sloping lanes cramped by eighteenth- and nineteenth-century fruit merchants' stone houses adorned with fancy grilles and big wooden doors. All streets lead to the main square, Plaça Constitució, an informal, pint-sized affair of crowded cafés and mopeds just down the hill from the train station. The square is dominated by the hulking mass of the church of St Bartomeu (Mon–Thurs 10.30am–1pm & 2.45–5.15pm, Fri & Sat 10.30am–1pm; free),

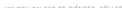
▼MUSEU BALEAR DE CIÉNCES, SÓLLER

▼PLAÇA CONSTITUCIÓ, SÓLLER

a crude but somehow rather fetching neo-Gothic remodelling of a medieval original – the most appealing features are the enormous and precisely carved rose window high in the main facade and the apparently pointless balustrade above it. Inside, the cavernous nave is suitably dark and gloomy, the penitential home of a string of gaudy Baroque altarpieces.

Five-minutes' walk west is the Museu Balear de Ciències Naturals (Balearic Museum of Natural Sciences; Tues–Sat 10am–6pm, Sun 10am–2pm; €3). Occupying an old merchant's house beside the main Palma–Sóller road, the interior has been stripped out to accommodate a series of modest displays. Temporary exhibitions occupy the top two floors and usually feature Balearic geology and fossils. The permanent collection is exhibited on the ground floor and is devoted

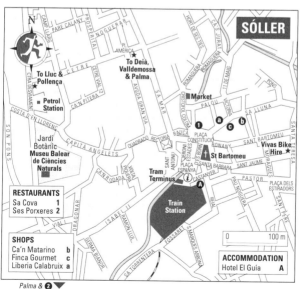

Palma & ❷ ▼

to the leading botanists of yesteryear, including Archduke Ludwig Salvator (see p.94). The labelling is in Catalan, but English leaflets are available at the ticket desk, which also issues a free English-language brochure identifying and illustrating many species of local flora. This is a necessary introduction to the neat and trim Jardí Botànic (same hours), which rolls down the hillside in front of the house. The garden is divided into thirteen small areas, including Balearic species such as shade-loving plants in M4, mountain plants in M5, and dune and sea-cliff species in M2.

Biniaraix and the Cornadors Circuit

Following c/Sa Lluna east from Sóller's main square, it takes about half an hour to stroll to the village of Biniaraix, passing orchards and farmland latticed with ancient irrigation channels and dry-stone walls. The village, nestled in the foothills of the Serra de Tramuntana, is tiny – just a cluster of handsome old stone houses surrounding a dilapidated church and the smallest of central squares – but it is extraordinarily pretty.

Biniaraix is also the starting point for one of Mallorca's busiest hiking routes, commonly called the Cornadors Circuit, which comprises a thirteen-kilometre trail that takes about six hours to negotiate, weaving a circuitous course through the mountains to finish up back in Sóller – although a local landowner has been restricting access to hikers beyond the Barranc de Biniaraix, so check with the Sóller tourist office in advance if you want to hike the whole circuit. To get to the trailhead, walk uphill from

▲ FORNALUTX

the square along c/Sant Josep. After about 200m you'll reach a spring and cattle trough, where a sign offers a choice of hiking routes: left for the Camí del Marroig, right for the Camí d'es Barranc, the first, and most diverting, part of the Cornadors Circuit. The Camí d'es Barranc follows an old cobbled track – originally built for pilgrims on their way to Lluc – which ascends the Barranc de Biniaraix, a beautiful gorge of terraced citrus groves set in the shadow of the mountains. After about ninety minutes' walking you'll reach the head of the ravine and a large barn sporting painted signs on its walls. Beyond this point the going gets appreciably tougher and the route more difficult to work out, so you'll need to have a hiking map with you. Otherwise, it's advisable to return the way you came.

Fornalutx

Fornalutx, a couple of kilometres east of Biniaraix along a narrow, signposted country lane, is often touted as the most attractive village on Mallorca, and it certainly has a superb location. Orange and lemon groves scent the valley as it tapers up towards the settlement, whose honey-coloured stone houses huddle against a mountainous backdrop. Matching its setting, the quaint centre of Fornalutx fans out from the minuscule main square, its narrow cobbled streets stepped to facilitate mule traffic, though nowadays you're more likely to be hit by a Mercedes than obstructed by a mule: foreigners love the place and own about half of the village's three hundred houses. This sizeable expatriate community sustains a clutch of cafés and restaurants and there are several enticing hotels, including the charming *Fornalutx Petit Hotel* (see p.103).

Port de Sóller

Port de Sóller is one of the most popular spots on the west coast, and its handsome, horseshoe-shaped bay, ringed by forested hills, must be one of the most photographed places on the island. The alcohol-fuelled high jinks of the Badia de Palma are a world away from this low-key, family-oriented resort, which is grafted onto an old fishing port and naval base. Attractions here include two pleasant strips of beach with generally clean and clear water, plus an excellent selection of restaurants. It's also worth making the enjoyable hour-long hike west to the lighthouse (*far*), which guards the cliffs of Cap Gros above the entrance to its inlet. From here, the views out over the wild and rocky coast and back across the harbour are truly magnificent, especially at sunset. There's a tarmac road all the way: from the tram terminus, walk round the southern side of the bay past Platja d'en Repic and keep going, following the signs.

Trams from Sóller (see p.86) shadow the main road and clank to a stop beside the jetties, bang in the centre of Port de Sóller. From here, it's a couple of minutes' walk east to the tourist office, located beside the church at c/Canonge Oliver 10 (Mon–Fri 9am–12.50pm & 2.40–4.50pm; ☎971 633042, Ⓦwww.sollernet.com), where you can pick up local information, including details of boat trips.

▼PORT DE SÓLLER

The Sa Firá i Es Firó

If you're around Port de Sóller in the second week of May, be sure to catch the Sa Firá i Es Firó, which commemorates the events of May 1561 when a large force of Arab pirates came to a sticky end after sacking Sóller. The Mallorcans had been taken by surprise, but they ambushed and massacred the Arabs as they returned to their ships and took grisly revenge by planting the raiders' heads on stakes. The story – bar decapitations – is played out in chaotic, alcoholic fashion every year at the festival. The re-enactment begins with the arrival of the pirates by boat, and continues with fancy-dress Christians and Arabs battling it out through the streets of the port, to the sound of blanks being fired in the air from antique rifles. The tourist office can give you a rough idea of the schedule of events, plus details of the dances and parties that follow.

The Jardins d'Alfàbia

Mon–Fri 9.30am–6.30pm, Sat 9.30am–1pm; Sept–May Mon–Fri 9.30am–5.30pm; €4.50. One of Mallorca's star turns, the Jardins d'Alfàbia are lush and beautiful terraced gardens set beside the southern entrance to the tunnel on the Palma–Sóller road. The gardens date back to the Spanish Reconquesta, when a prominent Moor by the name of Benhabet was gifted the Alfàbia estate in return for supporting the Jaume I invasion. Benhabet planned his new estate in the Moorish manner, channelling water from

▼JARDINS D'ALFÀBIA

the surrounding mountains to irrigate the fields and fashion oasis-like gardens. Generations of island gentry added to the estate without marring Benhabet's original design, thus creating the homogenous ensemble that survives today. From the roadside, you follow a stately avenue of plane trees towards the house. Before you reach it, you're directed up a flight of stone steps and into the gardens, where a footpath leads past ivy-covered stone walls, gurgling watercourses and brightly coloured flowers cascading over narrow terraces. Trellises of jasmine and wisteria create patterns of light and shade, while palm and fruit trees jostle upwards, allowing only the occasional glimpse of the surrounding citrus groves. At the end of the path, the gardens' highlight is a verdant jungle of palm trees, bamboo and bull-rushes tangling a tiny pool. It's an enchanting spot, especially on a hot summer's day, and an outdoor bar sells big glasses of freshly squeezed orange juice.

A few paces away is the house, a rather mundane, verandaed *hacienda* whose handful of rooms house an eccentric mix of antiques and curios. Pride of place goes to a superb fourteenth-century oak chair adorned with delightful bas-relief scenes depicting the story of Tristan and Isolde. At the front of the house, the cobbled courtyard is shaded by a giant plane tree and surrounded by good-looking, rustic outbuildings. Beyond lies the gatehouse, an imposing structure sheltering a fine coffered ceiling of Mudéjar design, with an inscription praising Allah.

If you fancy something to eat, the excellent *Restaurant Ses Porxeres* (see p.105) is right beside the gardens.

Bunyola and Orient

Just to the south of Alfàbia, a country road (the PM201 and then the PM210) forks east off the C711, looping past the plane trees and sun-bleached walls of the unassuming market town of Bunyola before snaking across the forested foothills of the Serra de Tramuntana. It's a beautiful (if occasionally nerve-jangling) drive and, after about 13km, you reach Orient, a remote hamlet of ancient houses scattered along the eastern side of the lovely Vall d'Orient. An especially beguiling spot, the village is framed by gentle hills covered with olive and almond groves and there's a superb hotel, the romantic *Hotel L'Hermitage* (see p.103).

The Castell d'Alaró

Beyond the *Hotel L'Hermitage*, the PM210 sticks to the ridge overlooking the narrow valley of the Torrent d'en Paragon for around 3km, before veering south to slip between a pair of molar-like hills whose bare rocky flanks tower above the surrounding forest and scrub. The more westerly of the two boasts the sparse ruins of the Castell d'Alaró, originally a Moorish stronghold but rebuilt by Jaume I. Visible for miles around, the castle looks impregnable on its lofty perch, and it certainly impeded the Aragonese invasion of 1285: when an Aragonese messenger suggested terms for surrender, the garrison's two commanders responded by calling the Aragonese king Alfonso III "fish-face", punning on his name in Catalan (*anfos* means "perch"). When the castle finally fell, Alfonso had the two roasted alive.

Access to the castle is from the south: coming from Orient, watch for the signposted right turn just beyond the Kilometre 18 stone marker. The first 3km of this narrow side road are well surfaced, but the last 1.3km is gravel and dirt, with a tight series of hairpins negotiating a

▼THE CASTELL D'ALARÓ

PLACES Western Mallorca

▲NOSTRA SENYORA DE ROBINES

very steep hillside – especially hazardous after rain. The road emerges at a car park and an old ramshackle farmstead, whose barn now holds the *Es Verger* restaurant. From the restaurant, the ruins of the castle are clearly visible and take about an hour to walk along a clearly marked track. The trail leads to the castle's stone gateway, beyond which lies an expansive wooded plateau accommodating the fragmentary ruins of the fortress, plus the tiny pilgrims' church of Mare de Déu del Refugi.

Alaró

Back on the PM210, it's about 1.5km south from the castle turn-off to the town of Alaró, a sleepy little place of old stone houses fanning out from an attractive main square, Plaça Vila. A long and elegant arcaded gallery flanks one side of the square, and a second is shadowed by the church, a fortress-like, medieval affair whose honey-coloured sandstone is embellished with Baroque details.

Binissalem

Long the centre of the island's wine industry, Binissalem is an appealing country town on the northern peripheries of Mallorca's central plain, Es Pla. It's true that Binissalem looks dull and ugly from the C713 Palma–Alcúdia road, but persevere: the tatty, semi-industrial sprawl that straddles the main road camouflages an antique town centre, whose narrow streets contain a proud ensemble of old stone mansions dating from the seventeenth and eighteenth centuries. The old town zeroes in on its main square, Plaça Església, a pretty, stone-flagged piazza shaded by plane trees. The north side of the square is dominated by the Església Nostra Senyora de Robines, the clumpy, medieval nave of which is attached to a soaring neo-Gothic bell tower added in 1908. Inside, the single-vaulted nave is dark and gloomy, its most distinctive features being its glitzy Baroque altarpiece and the grooved stonework, representing the cockleshell emblem of St James of Compostela – or the Greater – that graces the ceilings of the transepts and the apse.

Strolling southwest from the Plaça Església, along c/Concepció, it's a few metres to the Ajuntament (Town Hall), and five minutes more to Can Sabater, c/Bonaire 25, one of the town's most distinguished patrician mansions. This was once the home of the writer Llorenç Villalonga (1897–1980), whose most successful novel was *The Dolls' Room*, an ambiguous portrait of Mallorca's nineteenth-century landed gentry in moral decline. In his honour, the house has been turned into the Casa Museu Llorenç Villalonga (Mon–Sat 10am–2pm, also Tues & Thurs 4–8pm; free), with detailed Catalan explanations of his life and times as well as his library and study. It also has its own chapel: the island's richer families usually had their own live-in priests. Double back along c/Bonaire and take a right turn along c/Sant Vicenç de Paul, just before you reach the Ajuntament, to reach c/Pere Estruch, a cobbled street flanked by the town's most complete sequence of old stone houses, adorned by a medley of wooden shutters and wrought-iron balconies.

Buses to Binissalem pull in beside the C713 road at the foot of c/Bonaire, a five- to ten-minute walk from the Plaça Església. Binissalem is also on the train line from Palma to Manacor and Sa Pobla, and regular trains from both directions stop at the station on the northern edge of the town

centre. From the train station, it's a five- to ten-minute walk straight down c/S'Estació and right at the end along c/Porteta, to Passeig d'es Born beside the church on Plaça Església. Binissalem has no tourist office as such, but there are free town maps and brochures in the foyer of the Ajuntament – just help yourself. Binissalem also boasts one of Mallorca's finest hotels, *Scott's*, right in the centre of town at Plaça Església 12 – see p.103.

Deià

Deià, 10km west of Sóller, is beautiful. The mighty Puig d'es Teix (1062m) meets the coast here, and, although the mountain's lower slopes are now gentrified by the villas of the well-to-do, it retains a formidable, almost mysterious presence. Doubling as the coastal highway, Deià's main street, c/Arxiduc Lluís Salvador, skirts the base of the Teix, showing off most of the village's hotels and restaurants. Unfortunately, it's often too congested to be much fun, but the tiny heart of the village, tumbling over a high and narrow ridge on the seaward side of the road, still retains a surprising tranquillity. Here, labyrinthine alleys of old peasant houses curl up to a pretty country church, in the precincts of which is buried Robert Graves, the village's most famous resident. From the graveyard, there are memorable views out over the coast.

Graves put Deià on the international map, and nowadays the village is the haunt of long-term expatriates. Cala Deià, the nearest thing the village has to a beach, is some 200m of shingle at the back of a handsome rocky cove of jagged cliffs, boulders and

▼ROBERT GRAVES' TOMBSTONE, DEIÀ

Robert Graves in Deià

The English poet, novelist and classical scholar **Robert Graves** (1895–1985) had two spells of living in Deià, the first in the 1930s, and the second from the end of World War II until his death. During his first stay he lived with Laura Riding, an American poet and dabbler in the mystical. Married, the two had started their affair in England, where it created a furore, not as a matter of morality but because of its effects on the cabalistic and self-preoccupied literary-mystic group they had founded, the self-styled "Holy Circle". The last straw came when Riding, in her attempt to control the group, jumped out of a window, saying "Goodbye, chaps", and the besotted Graves leapt after her. The two both recovered, but the dottiness continued once they'd moved to Deià, with Graves acting as doting servant to Riding, whom he reinvented as a sort of all-knowing matriarch and muse. Simultaneously, Graves thumped away at his prose: he had already produced *Goodbye to All That* (1929), his bleak and painful memoirs of army service in the World War I trenches, but now came his other best-remembered books, *I, Claudius* (1934) and its sequel *Claudius the God* (1935), historical novels detailing the life and times of the Roman emperor.

At the onset of the Spanish Civil War, Graves and Riding left Mallorca to return to England, where Riding soon ditched Graves, who subsequently took up with a mutual friend, Beryl Hodge. Graves returned to Deià in 1946 and Hodge followed. They married in Palma in 1950, but did not live happily ever after. Graves had a predilection for young women, claiming he needed female muses for poetic inspiration, and although his wife outwardly accepted this waywardness, she did so without enthusiasm. Graves's international reputation ensured a steady stream of visitors to Deià from amongst the literati, but by the middle of the 1970s, Graves had begun to lose his mind, ending his days in senility in 1985.

white-crested surf. It's a great place for a swim, the water is clean, deep and cool, and there's a ramshackle beach bar. Most of the time, the cove is quiet and peaceful, but parties of day-trippers do sometimes stir things up. It takes about thirty minutes to walk from the village to the *cala*, a delightful stroll down a wooded ravine – the footpath is signed at the northeast end of the village opposite the *Restaurant El Olivo*. To drive there, head northeast along the main road out of Deià and watch for the (easy-to-miss) sign about 600m beyond the *El Olivo*.

Son Marroig

Mon–Sat: April–Sept 10am–7.30pm; Oct–March 10am–5.30pm; €3. South from Deià, the C710 snakes through the mountains for 3km to reach Son Marroig, an imposing L-shaped mansion perched high above the seashore – and just below the road. The house dates from late medieval times, but it was refashioned in the nineteenth century to become the favourite residence of the Habsburg archduke Ludwig Salvator (1847–1915). Dynastically insignificant but extremely rich, the Austrian noble was a man in search of a hobby – and he found it in Mallorca. He first visited the island at the age of 19, fell head-over-heels in love with the place, and returned to buy this chunk of the west coast. Once in residence, Ludwig immersed himself in all things *Mallorquín*, learning the dialect and chronicling the island's topography, archeology, history and folklore in astounding detail. The Son Marroig estate comprises the house, its gardens and the headland below. The house boasts a handful of period rooms, whose antique furnishings and fittings are enlivened by an eclectic sample of Hispano-Arabic pottery. On display too are some of the archduke's books and pen drawings, as well as several interesting photographs. The garden boasts gorgeous views along the jagged, forested coast and terraces graced by a Neoclassical belvedere of Tuscan Carrara marble.

Down below the garden is a slender promontory, known as Sa Foradada, "the rock pierced by a hole", where the archduke used to park his yacht. The hole in question is a strange circular affair, sited high up in the rock face at the end of the promontory. It takes about forty minutes to walk the 3km down to the tip of land, a largely straightforward excursion to a delightfully secluded and scenic spot. Before you set out, you need to get permission at the house – as the sign on the gate at the beginning of the path (up the hill and to the left of the house) insists.

Valldemossa

The ancient hill-town of Valldemossa is best approached from the south. Here, with the mountains closing in, the road squeezes through a narrow, wooded defile before entering a lovely valley, whose tiered and terraced fields ascend to the town, a sloping jumble of rusticated houses and monastic buildings backclothed by the mountains. The origins of Valldemossa date to the early fourteenth century, when the asthmatic King Sancho built a royal palace here in the hills where the air was easier to breathe. Later, in 1399, the palace was gifted to Carthusian monks from Tarragona, who converted and extended the original buildings into a monastery, now Mallorca's most visited building after Palma cathedral. The monastery has always dominated Valldemossa, but the rest of the town is exceptionally pretty, a jangle of narrow cobbled lanes that tumble prettily down the hillside. It only takes a few minutes to explore them and there are only two specific sights: the imposing Gothic bulk of the church of Sant Bartomeu and – round the back along a narrow alley, c/Rectoria 5 – the humble birthplace of Santa Catalina Thomàs, a sixteenth-century nun revered for her piety. The interior of the house has been turned into a simple little shrine, with a statue of the saint holding a small bird.

▼MONASTERY, VALLDEMOSSA

PLACES Western Mallorca

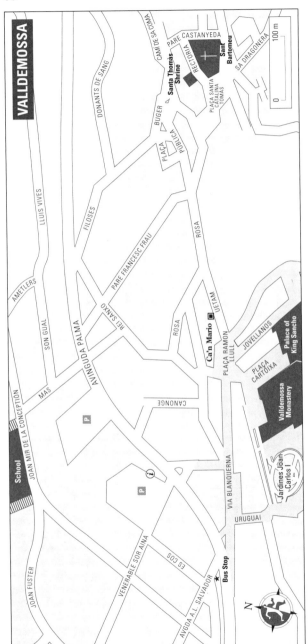

Valldemossa's Real Cartuja

March–Oct Mon–Sat 9.30am–6pm, Sun 10am–1pm; Nov–Feb Mon–Sat 9.30am–4.30pm; €7.50. Today's Real Cartuja de Jesús de Nazaret (Royal Carthusian Monastery of Jesus of Nazareth) is mostly of seventeenth- and eighteenth-century construction, having been remodelled on several occasions. It owes its present notoriety almost entirely to the novelist and republican polemicist George Sand (1804–76), who, with her companion, the composer Frédéric Chopin, lived here for four months in 1838–39. They arrived just three years after the last monks had been evicted during the suppression of the monasteries, and so were able to rent a commodious set of vacant cells. Their stay is commemorated in Sand's *A Winter in Majorca*, a quick-tongued and sharp-eyed epistle that is available hereabouts in just about every European language.

There's an obvious curiosity in looking around Sand's and Chopin's old quarters, but the monastery boasts far more interesting diversions, and it's easy to follow the multilingual signs around the place. A visit begins in the gloomy, aisle-less church, a square and heavy construction with a kitsch high altar and barrel vaulting that's distinguished by its late Baroque ceiling paintings. Beyond the church lie the shadowy cloisters, where the first port of call is the pharmacy crammed with beautifully decorated majolica jars, antique glass receptacles and painted wood boxes, each carefully inscribed with the name of a potion or drug. The nearby prior's cell is, despite its name, a comfortable suite of bright rooms, enhanced by access to a private garden with splendid views down the valley and graced by a wide assortment of religious *objets d'art*. Along the corridor, Cell no. 2 exhibits miscellaneous curios relating to Chopin and Sand, from portraits and a lock of hair to musical scores and letters. (It was in this cell that the composer wrote his "Raindrop" Prelude.) There's more of the same next door in Cell no. 4, plus Chopin's favourite piano which, after three months of unbelievable complications, only arrived just three weeks before the couple left for Paris. Considering the hype, these incidental mementoes are something of an anticlimax. Nor do things improve much in the ground-floor galleries of the adjacent Museu Municipal, which features local landscape painters. But don't give up: upstairs, the Museu Municipal Art Contemporani (same opening hours), holds a small but outstanding collection of modern art, including work by Miró, Picasso, Francis Bacon and Henry Moore, and a substantial sample of the work of the Spanish modernist Juli Ramís.

Back beside the prior's cell, be sure to take the doorway which leads outside the cloisters to the Palace of King Sancho. It's not the original medieval palace – that disappeared long ago – but this fortified mansion is the oldest part of the complex and its imposing walls, mostly dating from the sixteenth century, accommodate a string of handsome period rooms cluttered with faded paintings and other curios.

The palace has regular displays of folk dancing, and there are hourly free concerts of Chopin's piano music.

Port de Valldemossa

The closest spot to Valldemossa for a swim is Port de Valldemossa, a hamlet set in the shadow of the mountains at the mouth of a narrow, craggy cove. There's no public transport, but the drive down to the hamlet, once Valldemossa's gateway to the outside world, is stimulating: head west out of Valldemossa along the C710 and, after about 1.5km, turn right at the sign and follow the twisty side road for 6km through the mountains. Port de Valldemossa's beach is small and shingly, and tends to get battered by the surf, but the scenery is stunning and the village sports an excellent restaurant, the popular *Es Port* (see p.104).

La Granja

Daily: May–Sept 10am–7pm; Nov–March 10am–6pm; €9. Nestling in a wooded and terraced valley some 10km from Valldemossa, the house and extensive grounds of La Granja are a popular tourist trip, but nonetheless the estate has managed to maintain a languorous air of old patrician comfort. There's hardly anything new or modern on view here but somehow it doesn't seem contrived. La Granja was occupied until very recently by the Fortuny family, who took possession in the mid-fifteenth century, and, after about the 1920s, it seems that modernization simply never crossed their minds. The main house holds a ramshackle sequence of apartments strewn with domestic clutter – everything from children's games and mannequins, through old costumes, musical instruments to a cabinet of fans. There's also a delightful little theatre, where plays were once performed for the household in a manner common amongst Europe's nineteenth-century rural landowners. Likewise, the dining room, with its faded paintings and heavy drapes, has a real touch of country elegance, as does the graceful first-floor loggia. Look out also for the finely crafted, green-tinted Mallorcan chandeliers and the beautiful majolica tile-panels that embellish several walls.

Tagged onto the house, a series of workrooms recall the days when La Granja was a profitable and self-sufficient concern. A wine press, almond and olive-oil mills prepared the estate's produce for export, whilst plumbers, carpenters, cobblers, weavers and sail-makers all kept pace with domestic requirements from their specialized workshops. The main kitchen is in one of the cellars, where you'll also find a grain store and a "torture chamber", an entirely inap-

▼ LA GRANJA

propriate addition which holds a harrowing variety of instruments once regularly used by the Inquisition. Also of interest is the family chapel, a diminutive affair with kitsch silver-winged angels, and the expansive forecourt, which is surrounded by antiquated workshops, where costumed artisans practise traditional crafts. This part of the visit is a bit bogus, but good fun all the same – and the home-made pastries and doughnuts (*bunyols*) are lip-smacking.

Esporles

Esporles, just a couple of kilometres from La Granja, is an amiable, leafy little town whose elongated main street follows the line of an ancient stone watercourse. This is Mallorca away from the tourist zone, and although there's no special reason to stop, it's an attractive place to break any journey.

Puigpunyent and Galilea

Heading southwest from La Granja, a narrow and difficult country road heads up a V-shaped valley before snaking through the foothills of the Serra de Tramuntana mountains. After 10km you come to Puigpunyent, a workaday farmers' village cheered up by a seventeenth-century church with a squat bell tower. Continuing southwest, the road threads along a benign valley of citrus groves and olive trees before wriggling its way onto Galilea, an engaging scattering of whitewashed farmsteads built in sight of a stolid hilltop church. There's a rusty old café-bar beside the church, but the best place to soak up the bucolic atmosphere is at *Scott's Galilea* hotel (see p.103).

From Galilea, it's another short but tortuous-verging-on-the-

hair-raising drive to Andratx (see p.100).

Banyalbufar

The terraced fields of tiny Banyalbufar cling gingerly to the coastal cliffs beside the C710. The land here has been cultivated since Moorish times, with a spring above the village providing a water supply that's still channelled down the hillside along slender watercourses into open storage cisterns – themselves the unlikely-looking home for a few carp. The village is bisected by its main street, the C710, which is flanked by whitewashed houses and narrow cobbled lanes. They culminate in the cute main square, perched above the C710 and overlooked by a chunky parish church dating from the fifteenth century. The village is a fine place to unwind and there's a rough and rocky beach fifteen minutes' walk away down the hill – ask locally for directions since the lanes that lead there are difficult to find.

Estellencs

About 1km southwest of Banyalbufar stands perhaps the most impressive of the lookout points that dot the coastal road, the Mirador de Ses Ànimes, a sixteenth-century watchtower built as a sentinel against pirate attack and now providing stunning views along the coast. Estellencs, 6km further on, is similar to Banyalbufar, with steep coastal cliffs and tight terraced fields, though if anything it's even prettier. There's almost no sign of tourist development in the village, whose narrow, winding alleys are adorned with old stone houses and a trim, largely eighteenth-century parish church – peep inside for a look at the exquisite pinewood reredos. A steep, but driveable, two-kilometre lane leads down from the village, past olive and orange orchards, to Cala Estellencs, a rocky, surf-buffeted cove that shelters a shingly beach and a summertime bar.

The Mirador de Ricardo Roca and Andratx

Heading southwest from Estellencs, the C710 threads along the littoral for 6km before slipping through a tunnel and – immediately beyond – passing the stone stairway up to the Mirador de Ricardo Roca. At 400m above the sea, this lookout point offers some fine coastal views, and you can wet your whistle at the restaurant next door. Beyond the mirador, the C710 makes a few final flourishes before turning inland and worming its way up and over forested foothills to Andratx, a small and unassuming town where the main event is the Wednesday-morning market, a real tourist favourite. The old – and upper – part of Andratx is worth exploring, its medley of ancient stone houses and cobbled streets climbing up to the fortress-like walls of the parish church of Santa Maria, built high and strong to deter raiding pirates, its balustraded precincts offering panoramic views down to the coast.

Sant Elm and Sa Dragonera

Sa Dragonera Parc Natural. Daily: April–Sept 10am–5pm; Oct–March 10am–3pm. The low-key resort of Sant Elm is little more than one main street draped along the shore, with a sandy beach at one end and a tiny harbour at the other. It's not an especially pretty place to be sure, but there are frequent passenger ferries from its harbour to the austere offshore islet of Sa Dragonera, which is now protected as a Parc Natural.

The island, an uninhabited chunk of rock, some 4km long and 700m wide, lies at an oblique angle to the coast, with an imposing ridge of seacliffs dominating its northwestern shore. Most people visit for the scenic solitude, but the island is also good for birdlife: ospreys, shags, gulls and other seabirds are plentiful, and you may also see several species of raptor. Boats dock at Es Lladó, a tiny cove-harbour on the east side of the island, from where there's a choice of four walking trails: two are shortish strolls on the flatter, eastern side of the island, one is a stiff and steep jaunt up

▼CALA ESTELLENCS

▲ SANT ELM

into the seacliffs, and the final option is the bracing hoof to Cap des Llebeig lighthouse at the southern tip of the island – allow three to four hours for the whole excursion. Note, however, that you can't wander the island at will, so check permitted itineraries before you set out at the Es Lladó reception centre, or call ☎971 180632 ahead of time. The boat service is operated by Crucero Margarita (☎971 470449 or 696 423933; €8 return) with a timetable geared to the island's opening times; be sure to arrange your return trip on the way out.

Port d'Andratx

The picturesque port and fishing harbour of Port d'Andratx, 6km southwest of Andratx, has been transformed by a rash of low-rise shopping complexes and Spanish-style villas. However, the heart of the old town, which slopes up from the south side of the bay, preserves a cramped network of ancient lanes, and there's no denying the prettiness of the setting, with the port standing at the head of a long and slender inlet flanked by wooded hills. Sunsets show the place to best advantage, casting long shadows up the bay, and it's then that

the old town's gaggle of harbourside restaurants crowd with holidaymakers and expatriates, a well-heeled crew, occasionally irritated by raucous teenagers, who come here for the nightlife. All in all, Port d'Andratx is an enjoyable place to spend a night or two, especially as it possesses several outstanding seafood restaurants and is easy to reach. The one thing it doesn't have, however, is a sandy beach – the

▼ PORT D'ANDRATX

nearest one is east over the hills at Camp de Mar (see p.82).

Accommodation

Hostal Miramar

c/Ca'n Oliver s/n, Deià ☎ & ℗97163 9084. Pleasant one-star *hostal* above – and signposted from – the C710 about halfway through the village of Deià. The nine rooms here are fairly frugal, and not all of them are en suite, but the *hostal* occupies an attractive old stone building hidden away amongst the woods and olive groves that clamber up the hillside from the main road. Closed Nov–March. Shared bath €50, en suite €65.

Hostal Villa Verde

c/Ramón Llull, Deià 19 ☎971 639037, ℗971 639485. This lovely little *pension* perches on the side of a hill in the antique centre of Deià village, between the main road and the church. The rooms are immaculate and there's a charming shaded terrace overlooking Puig d'es Teix mountain. Closed Dec–Feb. €55.

Hotel Ca's Xorc

Ctra Sóller–Deià, km56.1 ☎971 638280, ⊛www.casxorc.com. Located high in the hills, about 5km west of Sóller along the C710, this wonderful hotel occupies a sympathetically modernized old olive mill with each guest room decorated in sleek modern style. There's an outside pool and handsome terraced gardens and the food is simply fabulous, featuring local ingredients and variations on traditional Mallorcan dishes. Reservations essential; closed mid-Nov to Feb. The smaller rooms start at €155, the most luxurious go for €280.

Hotel Costa d'Or

Llucalcari s/n, near Deià. ☎971 639025, ℗971 639347. This splendid one-star hotel, 2km east of Deià along the C710 coast road at the hamlet of Llucalcari, occupies a wonderful setting, overlooking an undeveloped slice of coast and surrounded by pine groves and olive terraces. There's a shaded terrace bar and a splendid outdoor swimming pool. The rooms vary, although all are spotlessly clean: there are some doubles in two buildings at the back of the complex, while the more expensive rooms look directly over the sea. Closed Nov–March. €65.

Hotel El Guía

c/Castanyer 3, Sóller. ☎971 630227, ℗971 632634. There are several glossy new hotels in Sóller, but this old-fashioned, one-star place, set back behind a pretty little courtyard, has been going for years and has oodles of character with bygones in the foyer and twenty simple but attractive rooms beyond. Handy location too – metres from the train station: to get there, walk down the steps from the station platform and turn right. Closed Nov–March. €70.

Hotel Es Moli

Carretera Valldemossa, Deià s/n ☎971 639000, ⊛www.hotelesmoli.com. One of Mallorca's most polished hotels, offering four-star luxury in a grand, lavishly refurbished old mansion overlooking the C710 at the west end of Deià village, surrounded by lovely gardens and equipped with a swimming pool. The ninety air-conditioned bedrooms are kitted out in dapper, modern style and most have balconies with sea views. Closed Nov to mid-April. The best rooms are a finger-burning €400 and more, but the least expensive are much more affordable at €200.

Hotel L'Hermitage

Ctra Alaró-Bunyola, Orient ☏971 180303, ⊛www.hermitage-hotel .com. In a luxuriously renovated medieval manor house roughly 1km east of Orient on the PM210, this top-flight hotel has lovely gardens, a fine rural setting, and an excellent restaurant, complete with a mammoth antique olive press. Advance reservations are pretty much essential and, if you're paying this sort of money, try to get one of the four rooms in the house, rather than one of the sixteen suites at the back. Closed early Nov to Jan. €185.

Hotel Marina

Passeig de Sa Platja 3, Port de Sóller ☏971 631461, ⊛www.hotelmarinasoller.com. Pleasant two-star hotel overlooking the Platja d'en Repic. The rooms are kitted out in brisk, modern style and most have bayside balconies. Closed mid-Nov to Jan. €80.

Petit Hotel

c/Alba 22, Fornalutx ☏971 631997, ⊛www.fornalutxpetithotel.com. This charming one-star hotel, with just eleven rooms, occupies an attractively furnished and spotlessly clean old stone house right in the centre of Fornalutx. The bonus is that the hotel's terraced garden has lovely views of the orchards behind. To get to c/Alba, walk down the main street from the village square and take the first left just beyond the conspicuous railings – a minute's stroll. €110.

Scott's Binissalem

Plaça Església 12, Binissalem ☏971 870100, ⊛www.scottshotel.com. One of Mallorca's finest hotels, *Scott's* sits right in the middle of Binissalem, a small town that has long been the centre of the island's wine industry. The hotel occupies an immaculately restored stone mansion that was originally owned by an almond grower, its sweeping stone arches and high ceilings enclosing three suites decorated in elegant, broadly nineteenth-century style. At the back, the old stone outbuildings surround a leafy courtyard and contain more recent rooms, each decorated in crisp modern style. Breakfast is served on a sunny terrace at the back of the hotel, and there's a swimming pool. Open all year. €175.

Scott's Galilea

Sa Costa den Mandons 3, Galilea ☏971 870100, ⊛www.scottsgalilea .com. The success of *Scott's Binissalem* has prompted the owner, George Scott, to open a new hotel on the edge of the tiny and remote mountain hamlet of Galilea. As before, the standards are immaculate – goosedown pillows, all-cotton sheets and so forth – and the *Galilea* offers superb mountain views with the ocean banding the horizon. €185.

Restaurants

Ca'n Mario

c/Uetam 8, Valldemossa ☏971 612122. In the *hostal* of the same name, this agreeable, family-run restaurant serves tasty traditional Mallorcan food at affordable prices – the (seasonal) asparagus with warm mayonnaise is a real treat. There's no sign – just go in through the *hostal* entrance and climb the stairs. The *hostal* is situated in a delightful old stone house just a minute's walk from Valldemossa monastery. Opening times are fairly elastic, which means you should make a reservation ahead of time.

▲ RESTAURANT ES CANYÍS

Restaurant Es Canyís

Passeig de Sa Platja d'en Repic 32, Port de Sóller ☎971 631406. Bright and cheerful bistro-style restaurant offering a good range of Spanish dishes from its bayshore premises behind the Platja d'en Repic. The snails are a house special. Main courses average €10–15. Closed Mon and mid-Dec to Feb.

Es Faro

Cap Gros, Port de Sóller ☎971 633752. Set in a wonderful location, high up on the cliffs at the entrance to the bay, the *Es Faro* offers coffee, light meals and an excellent *menú del día* during the day and à la carte at night with

main courses averaging €20–25. Reservations recommended. Closed Tues.

Restaurant Es Port

Port de Valldemossa ☎971 616194. Hidden away on the seashore, down at Port de Valldemossa, this first-rate restaurant has a well-deserved reputation for its superb seafood, with main courses from around €12. The paella is renowned across the island. Daily till 5 or 6pm.

Restaurant Es Racó d'es Teix

c/Vinya Vella 6, Deià ☎971 639501. Delightful Michelin-starred restaurant located in an old stone house with an exquisite shaded terrace, a steep 30m or so above the main road, about halfway into Deià – watch for the sign. The Mediterranean fusion cuisine is memorable and main courses range from €26–55. Reservations essential; closed Tues.

▼ RESTAURANT ES RACÓ D'ES TEIX

Restaurant Galicia

c/Isaac Peral 37, Port d'Andratx ☎971
672705. Highly recommended
Galician place serving mouth-
watering seafood without the
pretensions of some of its rivals
down on the harbourfront. Has
simple, traditional decor and
very reasonable prices. Closed
Mon & Jan.

Restaurant Jaime

c/Arxiduc Lluís Salvador 22, Deià ☎971
639029. First-rate restaurant, on
the main drag about halfway
into the village, specializing in
traditional Mallorcan cuisine;
dishes from around €12. Closed
Mon.

Restaurant Sa Cova

Plaça Constitució 7, Sóller ☎971
633222. Elegant and inviting
restaurant offering appetizing
versions of traditional Mallorcan dishes (from around €9),
including fish. Great location
too – on Sóller's main square.
Closed Mon.

Restaurant Sa Dorada

c/Arxiduc Lluís Salvador 24, Deià ☎971
639509. One of the best places
in Deià for fish, with main
courses from around €15. It's
located about halfway into the
village on the main road.

Restaurant Ses Porxeres

Carretera Sóller s/n, Sóller ☎971
613110. Something of an island
institution, this rustic restaurant
is well known for its game, prepared in the traditional Catalan
manner, along with other
Catalan-style dishes – reckon on
about €15 for a main course.
You'll need to reserve, and

note that on Sundays it can get
booked up weeks in advance. It's
located 4km from the centre of
Sóller, just beyond the south end
of the C711 Sóller tunnel beside
the Jardins d'Alfàbia. Closed Sun
eve & Mon.

Shopping

Bodega de José Luis Ferrer

c/Conquistador 103, Binissalem.
Mon–Fri 8am–7pm, Sat 10am–2pm;
☎971 511050. The biggest wine
producer on the island and the
maker of the best reds, José
Luis Ferrer operates this modest
bodega on the southern edge of
Binissalem. Call ahead for times
of tours and tastings (€6 per
person).

Ca'n Matarino

c/Sa Lluna 36, Sóller. Mon–Fri
10am–1pm & 4–7pm, Sat 10am–1pm.
The best butchers in Sóller
with all the usual offerings plus
home-made *sobrasada* (sausages)
and pates.

Finca Gourmet

c/Sa Lluna 16, Sóller. Mon–Fri
10am–1pm & 4–7pm, Sat 10am–1pm.
Smashing delicatessen featuring
all things Balearic from sausages
and pastries to bread, olives and
cheese.

Libreria Calabruix

c/Sa Lluna 7, Sóller. Mon–Fri
10am–1pm & 4–7pm, Sat 10am–1pm.
Facing the main square, this
is the best map shop in Sóller
– not much of a boast perhaps,
but if you forgot to buy a
walking map in Palma, they
should be able to assist.

Northern Mallorca

The magnificent Serra de Tramuntana mountains reach a precipitous climax in the rearing peaks that bump along the coast of northern Mallorca. This is the wildest part of the island where even today the ruggedness of the terrain forces the main coastal road to duck and weave inland, offering only the most occasional glimpse of the ocean. A rare exception is the extraordinary side road that snakes down to the attractive beach at Cala Tuent, as well as overcrowded Sa Calobra. But it's the well-appointed monastery of Lluc that remains the big draw here – for religious islanders and tourists alike.

Pushing on along the coast, the C710 emerges from the mountains to reach Pollença, a tangle of stone houses clustered around a fine, cypress-lined

Way of the Cross. This appealing town is also within easy striking distance of both the comely coastal resort of Cala Sant Vicenç and the wild and

rocky Península de Formentor, the bony, northernmost spur of the Serra de Tramuntana. The peninsula shelters the northern shore of the Badia de Pollença, where enjoyable Port de Pollença is a laid-back and family-oriented resort – in contrast to the more upbeat and flashy Port d'Alcúdia, hogging much of the next bay down, the Badia d'Alcúdia. In its turn, this port-resort is close to the old, walled town of Alcúdia, where there is a clutch of modest historical sights, and pocket-sized Muro, with its splendid main square and church. Back on the coast, the flow of the resorts is interrupted by the Parc Natural de S'Albufera, which takes the prize as the best birdwatching

wetland in Mallorca. As regards beaches, there are long golden strands stretching round the bays of Pollença and Alcúdia and pretty cove beaches at Cala Sant Vicenç.

Gorg Blau

Heading northeast from Sóller, the C710 zigzags up into the mountains. After about 5km, it passes the steep turning down to Fornalutx (see p.89) before offering a last lingering look over the coast from the Mirador de Ses Barques. Thereafter, the road snakes inland and tunnels through the western flanks of Puig Major (1447m), the island's highest mountain. Beyond the tunnel is the Gorg Blau (Blue Gorge), a bare and bleak

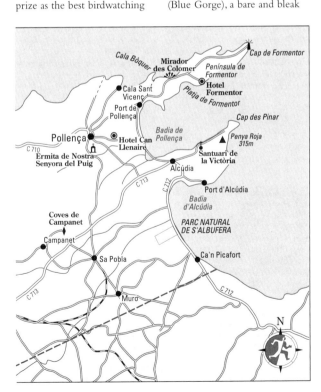

ravine that was a well-known beauty spot until a hydroelectric scheme filled it with puddle-like reservoirs. One of them is the Embalse de Cúber, an unappetizing expanse of water redeemed by its abundant birdlife, notably several different types of raptor. For a better look, follow the easy footpath which circumnavigates the reservoir; it takes a couple of hours to complete.

To the immediate north rear the craggy flanks of Puig Major, but the dramatic trail which twists up towards the summit from the military base beside the main road remains off-limits because of its radar station. This makes Puig de Massanella (1367m), which looms over the gorge to the east, the highest mountain that can be climbed on the whole of the island.

Cala Tuent

At the far end of the Gorg Blau the road tunnels into the mountains, to emerge just short of a left turn leading to Cala Tuent and Sa Calobra (see below). This turn-off makes for an exhilarating, ear-popping detour to the seashore, the well-surfaced road

hairpinning its way down the mountain slopes so severely that at one point it actually turns 270 degrees to run under itself. About 10km down this road, there's a fork: head left over the hills for the 4km journey to the Ermita de Sant Llorenç, a tiny medieval church perched high above the coast, and Cala Tuent, where a smattering of villas cling to the northern slopes of Puig Major as it tumbles down to the seashore. Ancient orchards temper the harshness of the mountain, and the gravel and sand beach is one of the quietest on the north coast. It's a lovely spot to while away a few hours – if you can wrangle a parking spot (space is extremely limited) – and the swimming is safe provided you stay close to the shore.

Sa Calobra

Sa Calobra is a modern resort occupying a pint-sized cove in the shadow of the mountains. The setting itself is gorgeous, but the place is an over-visited disaster, and you'll have to pay €4 just to park. Almost every island operator deposits a busload of tourists here every

▼ROAD TO SA CALOBRA

day in summer and the crush is quite unbearable – as is the overpriced and overcooked food at the local cafés. The reason why so many people come here is to visit the impressive box canyon at the mouth of the Torrent de Pareis (River of the Twins). It takes about ten minutes to follow the partly tunnelled walkway round the coast from the resort to the mouth of the canyon. Here, with sheer cliffs rising on every side, the milky-green river trickles down to the narrow bank of shingle that bars its final approach to the sea – though the scene is transformed after heavy rainfall, when the river crashes down into the canyon and out into the sea.

▲ MONESTIR DE LLUC

Monestir de Lluc

Daily: April–Sept 10am–11pm; Oct–March 10am–8pm; free. Tucked away in a remote valley about 35km northeast of Sóller, the austere, high-sided dormitories and orange-flecked roof tiles of the Monestir de Nostra Senyora de Lluc (Monastery of Our Lady of Lluc) stand out against the greens and greys of the surrounding mountains. It's a magnificent setting for what has been Mallorca's most important place of pilgrimage since the middle of the thirteenth century, when a local shepherd boy named Lluc stumbled across a tiny, brightly painted statue of the Virgin in the woods.

At the centre of the complex – pass through the monastery's double-doored entrance and keep straight on to the second courtyard – is the main shrine and architectural highlight, the Basílica de la Mare de Déu de

Lluc. Here, the basilica's elegant Baroque facade precedes a dark and gaudily decorated interior, dominated by heavy jasper columns. On either side of the nave, stone steps extend the aisles round the back of the Baroque high altar to a small chapel. This is the holy of holies, built to display Luke's statue of the Virgin, which has been commonly known as La Moreneta ("the Little Dark-Skinned One") ever since the original paintwork peeled off in the fifteenth century to reveal brown stone underneath. Just 61cm high, the Virgin looks innocuous, her face tweaked by a hint of a smile and haloed by a much more modern jewel-encrusted gold crown. In her left arm she cradles a bumptious baby Jesus, who holds the "Book of Life", open to reveal the letters alpha and omega.

Every day, during the 11am mass and again at around 7pm, the Escolania de Lluc, a boys' choir founded in the early sixteenth century with the stipulation that it must be "composed of natives of Mallorca, of pure blood, sound in grammar and song", performs in the basilica. They're nicknamed *Ses Blavets*, "The Blues", for the colour of their cassocks.

Museu de Lluc

Daily: 10am–1.30pm & 2.30–5.15pm; €2.50. Just inside and to the right of the monastery's main entrance a stairway climbs up to the enjoyable Museu de Lluc (Lluc Museum). After a modest section devoted to archeological finds from the Talayotic and Roman periods comes an assortment of exquisite gold and silver sacred vessels plus a selection of votive offerings, bits and bobs brought here to honour La Moreneta.

Upstairs, the highlight is the extensive collection of majolica (see box below), glazed earthenware, mostly shaped into two-handled drug jars and show dishes or plates. The designs vary in sophistication from broad and bold dashes of colour to carefully painted naturalistic designs, but the colours remain fairly constant, restricted by the available technology to iron red, copper green, cobalt blue,

manganese purple and antimony yellow. There are also some rare examples of Islamic lustreware.

On the same floor is a large but patchy selection of minor Mallorcan and Spanish paintings amongst which the romantic island scenes of Bartomeu Sureda (1769–1851) and the finely executed mountain landscapes of Antoni Ribas (1845–1911) are the most engaging. A separate section is devoted to sentimental work of the early twentieth-century artist José Coll Bardolet.

Lluc's Camí dels Misteris del Rosari

From outside the monastery's double-doored entrance, walk a few metres to the west and you'll soon spot the large, rough-hewn column at the start of the Camí dels Misteris del Rosari (Way of the Mysteries of the Rosary), a broad pilgrims' footpath that winds its way up the rocky hillside directly behind the monastery. Dating from 1913, the solemn granite stations marking the route are of two types: simple stone pediments and, more intriguingly, rough trilobate columns of Gaudí-like design,

Majolica

The fifteenth century witnessed a vigorous trade in decorative pottery sent from Spain to Italy via Mallorca. The Italians coined the term "*majolica*" to describe this imported Spanish pottery after the medieval name for the island through which it was traded, but thereafter the name came to be applied to all tin-glazed pottery. The process of making majolica began with the mixing and cleaning of clay, after which it was fired and retrieved at the "biscuit" (earthenware) stage. The biscuit was then cooled and dipped in a liquid glaze containing tin and water. The water in the glaze was absorbed, leaving a dry surface ready for decoration. After painting, the pottery was returned to the kiln for a final firing, which fused the glaze and fixed the painting. Additional glazings and firings added extra lustre. Initially, majolica was dominated by greens and purples, but technological advances added blue, yellow and ochre in the fifteenth century. Majolica of one sort or another was produced in Mallorca up until the early twentieth century.

each surmounted by a chunky crown and cross. The prettiest part of the walk is round the back of the hill where the path slips through the cool, green woods with rock overhangs on one side and views out over the bowl-shaped Albarca valley on the other. It takes about ten minutes to reach the top of the hill, where a wrought-iron *Modernista* cross stands protected by ugly barbed-wire. Afterwards it's possible to stroll down into the Albarca valley by following the country road that begins to the left of the monastery's main entrance. The valley is shadowed by Puig Roig (1002m), but there's nowhere in particular to aim for and the road fizzles out long before you reach the coast.

Lluc's Jardí Botànic

Same hours as monastery; free.
On the right hand side of the main complex – just follow the signs – lie the monastery's botanical gardens (Jardí Botànic). Dense and lush, the gardens are traversed by a foot-path that clambers up the hill passing local plants as well as exotics, with small ponds and waterfalls, little footbridges and a stone shed that serves as a tiny museum for antique tools, ancient household crockery and the like.

Pollença

The lovely little town of Pol-lença nestles among a trio of humpy hillocks where the coastal mountains fade into flatland some 20km from Lluc. Follow-ing standard Mallorcan practice, the town was established a few kilometres from the seashore to militate against sudden pirate attack, with its harbour, Port de Pollença (see p.114), left unpro-tected. For once the stratagem

worked. Pollença successfully repelled a string of piratical onslaughts and the dignified stone houses that cramp the twisting lanes of the centre today date back to the seventeenth and eighteenth centuries.

In the middle, Plaça Major, the amiable main square, accommo-dates a cluster of laid-back cafés and is the site of a lively Sunday-morning fruit and veg market. Overlooking the square is the severe façade of the church of Nostra Senyora dels Àngels, a sheer cliff-face of sun-bleached stone pierced by a rose window. Close by, behind the church on the north side of the centre, is Pollença's pride and joy, its Via Crucis (Way of the Cross), a long, steep and beautiful stone stairway, graced by ancient cypress trees which ascends El Calvari (Calvary Hill). At the top, a much-revered statue of Mare de Déu del Peu de la Creu

PLACES Northern Mallorca

▼PLAÇA MAJOR, POLLENÇA

Northern Mallorca **PLACES**

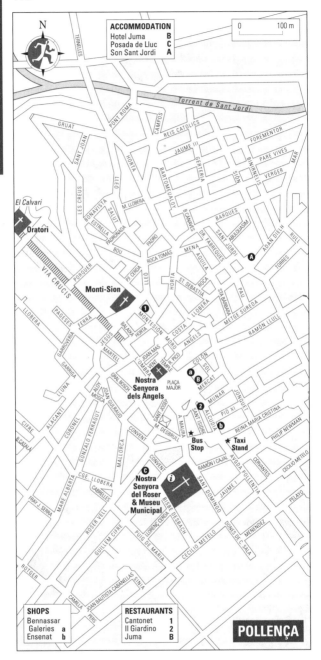

▲ POLLENÇA MARKET

(Mother of God at the Foot of the Cross) is lodged in a simple, courtyarded *oratori* (chapel), from where the views out over the coast and town are sumptuous. On Good Friday, a figure of Jesus is slowly carried by torch-light down from the *oratori* to the aforementioned church of Nostra Senyora, a solemn and moving procession known as the *Davallament* (Lowering).

On the south side of the centre, along c/Antoni Maura, stands the deconsecrated church of Nostra Senyora del Roser, whose cloisters hold the Museu Municipal (July–Sept Tues–Sat 10.30am–1.30pm & 5.30–8.30pm, Sun 10am–1pm; Oct–June Tues–Sun 11am–1pm; €1.50). This holds a compelling collection of contemporary paintings, photography and video art as well as local archeological finds, ecclesiastical bric-a-brac, and several good examples of Mallorcan Primitive art.

Ermita de Nostra Senyora del Puig

There are magnificent views from the Ermita de Nostra Senyora del Puig, a rambling, mostly eighteenth-century monastery perched on top of the Puig de Maria, a 320-metre-high hump facing the south

end of Pollença. The monastic complex, with its fortified walls, courtyard, chapel, refectory and cells, has had a chequered history, alternately abandoned and restored by both monks and nuns. The Benedictines now own the place, but the monks are gone and today a custodian supplements the order's income by renting out cells to tourists (see p.121). There's nothing specific to see, but the setting is extraordinarily serene and beautiful, with the mellow honey-coloured walls of the monastery surrounded by ancient carob and olive trees, a million miles from the tourist resorts visible far below.

It takes around an hour to walk to the monastery from the centre of town. Take the signposted turning off the main Pollença–Inca road just south of town and head up this steep lane until it fizzles out after 1.5km, to be replaced by a cobbled footpath which winds up to the monastery's entrance. It's possible to drive to the top of the lane, but unless you've got nerves of steel, you're better off parking elsewhere. Note that there have been reports of cars left overnight at the foot of the lane being vandalized; although this is unusual, you might prefer to park in town instead.

Cala Sant Vicenç

One of Mallorca's more agreeable resorts, Cala Sant Vicenç, 6km northeast of Pollença, boasts an attractive, solitary setting, its medley of well-heeled villas and modern hotels gambolling over and around a wooded ravine just behind a pair of pint-sized sandy beaches. The fly in the aesthetic ointment is the overpowering *Hotel Don Pedro*, insensitively located on the minuscule headland separating the beaches. But, the resort is still a pleasant spot for a swim – the water is crystal clear and the beach is sheltered from the wind.

In addition, you can hike out onto the wild and wind-licked seashore that extends to either side of the resort. One tempting option is the moderately strenuous hoof north up the adjoining headland to the top of Puig de l'Àguila (206m), from where there are grand views over the surrounding coast and back over the resort. This six-kilometre hike takes around three hours; the first part uses a rough stone road, the second follows a well-defined path which leads to the base of Puig de l'Àguila – but you'll still need a proper hiking map to find your way.

Port de Pollença

With the mountains as a shimmering backcloth, Port de Pollença is a pleasantly low-key, family-oriented resort, which arches through the flatlands behind the Badia de Pollença, a deeply indented bay whose sheltered waters are ideal for swimming. The beach is the focus of attention, a narrow, elongated sliver of sand that's easily long enough to accommodate the crowds, though as a general rule you'll have more space the further south (towards Alcúdia) you go. A rash of apartment buildings and hotels blights the edge of town, but there are no high-rises to speak of and the resort is dotted with attractive whitewashed and stone-trimmed villas. All together it's simply delightful, especially to the north of the marina, where a portion of the old beachside road – along Passeig Anglada Camarasa – has been pedestrianized.

The flatlands edging the Badia de Pollença and stretching inland as far as Pollença and along the bay to Alcúdia make for easy, scenic cycling. Bikes can be rented from March, c/ Joan XXIII, 89 (☎971 864784), as can mopeds and motorcycles. In addition, passenger ferries shuttle between the marina and

▼CALA SANT VICENÇ

the Platja de Formentor (see p.115), one of Mallorca's most attractive beaches (April–Oct 5 daily; 30min; €7.50 return) and boat trips cruise the bay.

The Península de Formentor

Heading northeast out of Port de Pollença, the road clears the military zone at the far end of the resort before weaving up into the hills at the start of the twenty-kilometre-long Península de Formentor, the final spur of the Serra de Tramuntana. At first, the road – which suffers a surfeit of tourists from mid-morning to mid-afternoon – offers extravagant views back over the Badia de Pollença, but this is merely a foretaste of what lies beyond. The first place to stop, about 4km from town, is the Mirador des Colomer, where a string of lookout points perch on the edge of plunging, north-facing seacliffs.

Pushing on, it's five kilometres more to the large car park at the far end of the Platja de Formentor, a long and slender pine-clad beach of golden sand. It's a beautiful spot, with views over to the mountains on the

far side of the bay, though it can get a little crowded. There are buses to the beach, but the best way to get here is by passenger ferry from Pollença (April–Oct 5 daily; 30min; €7.50 return).

Also at the west end of the beach, approached along its own access road, is the *Hotel Formentor*, one of the island's finest hotels (see p.121). Beyond the hotel turn-off, the main peninsula road runs through woods before clambering upwards, tunnelling through Mont Fumat to emerge on the rocky mass of the Cap de Formentor, a tapered promontory of bleak seacliffs and scrub-covered hills. From the silver-domed lighthouse stuck on the cape's windswept tip, there are magnificent views and good birdwatching. Ravens, martins and swifts often circle overhead and during the spring and summer migrations, thousands of seabirds fly over the cape, Manx and Cory's shearwaters in particular. If you fancy a snack before heading back from the cape, there's a (very average) café in part of the lighthouse.

▼THE PENÍNSULA DE FORMENTOR

Alcúdia

To pull in the day-trippers, pint-sized Alcúdia wears its history on its sleeve. The crenellated wall that encircles much of the town centre is a modern restoration of the original medieval defences, and although the sixteenth- to eighteenth-century town houses behind it are genuine enough, the whole place is inordinately spick and span. Situated on a neck of land separating two large and sheltered bays, the site's strategic value was first recognized by the Phoenicians, who settled here in around 700 BC, but they were displaced by the Romans, who built their island capital, Pollentia, on top of the earlier settlement. The Moors built a fortress here in about 800, naming it Al Kudia (On the Hill), and thereafter the town prospered as a trading centre, a role it performed well into the nineteenth century, when the town slipped into a slow decline – until tourism refloated the local economy.

It only takes an hour or so to explore Alcúdia's compact centre, beginning at the old town's eastern entrance, on Plaça Carles V, from where you'll soon reach the tiny main square, Plaça Constitució and its pavement cafés. Just beyond, on c/Major, is Alcúdia's best-looking building, the Ajuntament (Town Hall), a handsome, largely seventeenth-century structure with an elegant stone balcony and overhanging eaves.

From c/Major, it's a brief walk to the southwest corner of the old town and the fascinating Museu Monogràfic, c/Sant Jaume 2 (Tues–Fri 10am–3.30pm, Sat & Sun 10.30am–12.45pm; €2, which includes admission to the Pollentia ruins – see below). The museum consists of just one large room, but it's stuffed with a satisfying assortment of archeological bits and bobs, primarily Roman artefacts from Pollentia, including amulets, miniature devotional objects, tiny oil lamps and, remarkably enough, a gladiator's helmet. Across the street, dominating this portion of the old town, is the heavyweight and heavily reworked Gothic church of Sant Jaume, which holds a modest religious museum (Tues–Fri 10am–1pm; €1).

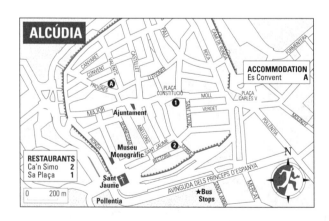

Alcúdia's Roman ruins

Across the ring road from the church of Sant Jaume lie the broken pillars and mashed-up walls of Roman Pollentia (same times and ticket as the Museu Monogràfic). The Vandals ransacked the Roman city in 426 and thereafter the locals helped themselves to the rest of the stone, so it takes a lot of imagination to discern the layout of the former capital, though the signs do their best. By contrast, the open-air remains of the Teatre Romà (Roman Theatre; open access; free) are much more substantial. Dating from the first century BC, this is the smallest of the twenty Roman theatres to have survived in Spain. Nonetheless, despite its modest proportions, the builders were able to stick to the standard type of layout with eight tiers of seats carved out of the rocky hillside, divided by two gangways. Inevitably, the stage area, which was constructed of earth and timber, has disappeared, but getting the flavour of the place is easy enough. It's a pleasant spot too, the ruins set amidst fruit and olive trees, a ten-minute stroll to the south of the old town. The short, signed footpath to the Roman theatre leads along c/Santa Anna, a pretty country lane lined by old stone walls that runs south from the ring road a couple of hundred metres east of the remains of Pollentia.

The Santuari de la Victòria

East of Alcúdia a steep and rocky promontory pokes a wild finger out into the ocean, the first part of its northern shore traversed

▲ALCÚDIA TOWN WALLS

by a narrow road which begins at the easternmost intersection on Alcúdia's ring road. This promontory road slips past the marina and suburban villas of Bonaire before emerging into more scenic terrain, offering fine views of the Badia de Pollença as it bumps over the steep, pine-clad ridges that fringe the coast. After about 5km, a signed turning on the right climbs 600m up the wooded hillside to the Santuari de la Victòria, a fortress-like church with a simple, single vault nave, built in the seventeenth century to hold and protect a crude, but much-venerated, statue of the Virgin. It was a necessary precaution: this part of the coast was especially prone to attack and, even with these defences, pirates still stole the statue twice, though on both occasions the islanders eventually got it back. Part of the

PLACES

Northern Mallorca

▲PORT D'ALCÚDIA BEACH

Santuari has been turned into an excellent and inexpensive hotel (see p.121) and there's a first-rate restaurant here too (see p.123). Furthermore, the Santuari is the starting point for hikes further along the promontory, whose severe peaks are dotted with ruined defensive installations. The obvious draw is the 315-metre Penya Roja mountain, from whose summit there are more great views. The outward part of the hike, leading up through woods and beneath steep cliffs, is quite strenuous; return is by the same route. Allow thirty to forty-five minutes each way. It begins on the wide dirt road that climbs up behind the Santuari, but the later sections are on trails that require a hiking map.

Port d'Alcúdia

Port d'Alcúdia, 2km south of Alcúdia, is easily the biggest and busiest of the resorts in the north of the island, a seemingly interminable string of high-rise hotels and apartment buildings serviced by myriad restaurants and café-bars. Despite the superficial resemblance, however, Port d'Alcúdia is a world away from the seamy resorts of the Badia de Palma: the tower blocks are relatively well distributed, the streets are neat and tidy, and there's a prosperous and easygoing air, with families particularly well catered for. Predictably, the daytime focus is the beach, a superb arc of pine-studded golden sand which stretches south round the Badia d'Alcúdia from the two purpose-built jetties of Port d'Alcúdia's combined marina, cruise boat and fishing harbour. A tourist "train" (on wheels) runs up and down the length of the resort every hour from June to September, transporting sunbaked bodies from one part of the beach to another. Not that there's very much to distinguish anywhere from anywhere else – the numbered palm-thatched *balnearios* (beach bars) are a great help in actually remembering where you are. A walkway runs along the back of the beach, which is usually more crowded to the north.

Just as crowded, and located a kilometre or so inland along Avinguda del Tucan, is the much-vaunted Hidropark, a gigantic pool complex with all sorts of flumes and chutes (May–Oct daily 10am–6pm; €14). There's a superabundance of car, moped and bike rental companies strung out along the main drag, the Carretera d'Artà, and summer boat trips, leaving from the marina, make frequent explorations of the rocky, mountainous coastline to the northeast.

The Parc Natural de S'Albufera

☎971 892250. Daily: April–Sept 9am–6pm; Oct–March 9am–5pm; free. Given all the high-rise development along the Badia d'Alcúdia, the pristine wetland of the 2000-acre Parc Natural de S'Albufera makes a wonderful change. Swampland once extended round much of the bay, but large-scale reclamation began in the nineteenth century, when a British company dug a network of channels and installed a steam engine to pump the water out. These endeavours were prompted by a desire to eradicate malaria – then the scourge of the local population – as much as by the need for more farmland. Further drainage schemes accompanied the frantic tourist boom of the 1960s, and only recently has the Balearic government organized a park to protect what little remains.

The park entrance is clearly signposted on the C712, about 6km southeast of Port d'Alcúdia's marina. From the entrance, a country lane leads just over 1km inland to the reception centre, Sa Roca, where you can pick up a free map, a permit and a list of birds you might see. There's a small wildlife display here too, and an adjacent building houses a second flora and fauna identity parade. Note that you can't drive down the country lane; the best bet is to cycle here or take a bus to the entrance and walk – lots of buses from Port d'Alcúdia stop near the entrance. If you do bring a vehicle, there's a dedicated parking area at the conspicuous *Hotel Parc Natural*. The hotel is located a few metres east of – and opposite – the park entrance.

Footpaths and cycle trails head out from Sa Roca into the reedy, watery tract beyond, where a string of well-appointed hides allow excellent birdwatching. Over 200 different types of birds have been spotted, including resident wetland-loving birds from the crake, warbler and tern families; autumn and/or springtime migrants such as grebes, herons, cranes, plovers and godwits; and wintering egrets and sandpipers. Such rich pickings attract birds of prey in their scores, especially kestrels and harriers.

PLACES Northern Mallorca

▼ PARC NATURAL DE S'ALBUFERA

Muro

Heading east from the Parc Natural de S'Albufera on the C712, it's the briefest of drives to the gentle country road that slips inland across the pancake-flat, windmill-studded landscape that prefigures the hilltop town of Muro, a sleepy little place dotted with big old town houses built by wealthy landowners. The best time to be here is on the Revetla de Sant Antoni Abat (Eve of St Antony's Day), January 16, when locals gather round bonfires to drink and dance, tucking into specialities like sausages and eel pies (*espinagades*).

At other times of the year, allow an hour or two to explore the town, beginning with its handsome main square, Plaça Constitució, an attractive open area flanked by old stone houses. The square is also overseen by the ponderous hulk of the church of St Joan Baptista, a real hotchpotch of architectural styles, its monumental Gothic lines uneasily modified by the sweeping sixteenth-century arcades above the aisles. A slender arch connects the church to the adjacent belfry, an imposing seven-storey construction partly designed as a watchtower. The church's cavernous interior holds a mighty vaulted roof and an immense altarpiece, a flashy extravaganza of columns, parapets and tiers in a folksy rendition of the Baroque.

From the main square, it's a couple of minutes' walk east to the Museu Etnològic, c/Major 15 (Tues–Sat 10am–3pm & Sun 10am–2pm; €2.40), set in a rambling old mansion and displaying a motley assortment of local bygones, such as old agricultural implements and traditional costumes. Among the pottery, look out for the *siurells*, miniature white-, green- and red-painted figurines created in a naive style. Now debased as a mass-produced tourist trinket, they were originally made as whistles – hence the spout with the hole – shaped in the form of animals, humans and mythological or imaginary figures. That's just about it for Muro, though on a hot summer's day you'll be glad of a drink at one of the cafés around the main square.

Sa Pobla

From Muro, it's just 4km northwest to the dusty little agricultural town of Sa Pobla, whose straightforward grid-iron of old streets is at its prettiest in the main square, the Plaça Constitució, which is also the site of a busy Sunday-morning market.

Also of interest is Can Planes, c/Antoni Maura 6 (Tues–Sat 10am–2pm & 4–8pm, Sun 10am–2pm; €4), a late nineteenth-century *Modernista* mansion which has been turned into a cultural centre incorporating a contemporary art gallery and toy museum. The mansion is poorly signed and can be hard to find – it's located at the north end of c/Antoni Maura (which runs north–south across the west side of the town centre), close to its intersection with Carretera Inca, the main road to Inca. The gallery's permanent collection features the work of Mallorcan and foreign artists resident on the island since the 1970s and there's an ambitious programme of temporary exhibitions too. Upstairs, the toy museum holds an assortment of nineteenth- and early to mid-twentieth-century toys and games – some four thousand exhibits in all, from miniature rocking horses and carousels to baffling board games.

Accommodation

Ermita de Nostra Senyora del Puig

Puig Maria, Pollença ☎971 184132. Ten of the original monks' cells here have been renovated to provide simple rooms sleeping between two and four guests. There's also space for thirty on the floor of another room, but in this case you have to bring your own sleeping bag and you don't save any money – the price is the same. All guests have access to shared showers and there's a refectory, but the food is only average. Most guests turn up on spec: to be sure of a room, book ahead. Be warned that the trek up to the monastery is a real lung-wrencher and note also that it can get cold and windy at night, even in the summer. The Puig Maria is 12km south of Pollença; for a description of the former monastery, see p.113. €6 per person.

Hostal Bahía

Passeig Voramar 31, Port de Pollença ☎971 866562, ℻971 865630. In a lovely location a few minutes' walk north of the marina along the (pedestrianized part of the) seafront, this pleasant, unassuming one-star *hostal* offers thirty rooms in one of the port's older villas. Closed Nov–March. €100.

Hostatgeria Santuari de la Victòria

Santuari de la Victòria, near Alcúdia ☎971 549912, ℻971 547173. The church at the Santuari de la Victòria remains unchanged (see p.117), but the old monastic quarters behind and above it have been imaginatively converted into a charming *hostal*. This has twelve en-suite guest rooms decorated in a suitably frugal, but highly buffed and polished style. Highly recommended and a snip at €60.

Hotel Can Llenaire

Carretera Llenaire ☎971 535251, ⓦwww.hotelllenaire.com. This imposing Mallorcan manor house sits on the brow of a hill with wide views over the Badia de Pollença, the mountains glinting in the distance. The owner still runs the surrounding land as a farm, with sheep grazing and groves of almond and olive trees, but the house has been turned into a charming hotel with most of the original architectural features, dating back to the eighteenth century, sympathetically renovated. There are just eleven rooms, each decked out in period style. The hotel is clearly signposted down a country lane from the main coastal road just east of the centre of Port de Pollença. €210.

Hotel Es Convent

c/Progrés 6, Alcúdia ☎971 548716, ⓦwww.esconvent.com. Right in the centre of Alcúdia, this charming hotel occupies an exquisitely restored medieval building, all beamed ceilings, bare stone walls and arches. Modern additions are minimalist, with lots of whites and creams, and this applies in equal measure to the four guest bedrooms. The restaurant here is excellent too, featuring local ingredients and local dishes. €90.

Hotel Formentor

Platja de Formentor ☎971 899100, ⓦwww.hotelformentor.net. Opened in 1930, this grand old hotel – in its heyday the island's best – lies low against the forested hillside, its *hacienda*-style architecture enhanced by Neo-classical and Art Deco features and exquisite terraced gardens. The place was once the haunt of the rich and fashionable – Charlie Chaplin and F. Scott Fitzgerald both stayed here – and although its socialite days are long gone, the hotel preserves an air of understated elegance. It has every facility, and dinner is served on an outside terrace perfumed by the flowers of the gardens; breakfast is taken on the splendid upper-floor loggia with spectacular views over the bay. The rooms are not quite as grand as you might expect, but are still charming. Stay here if you can afford it; there's a good chance of a vacant room, even in high season. €250.

Hotel Juma

Plaça Major 9, Pollença ☎971 535002, ⓦwww.hoteljuma.com. First-rate, three-star hotel occupying a smart and tastefully converted old merchant's stone house in the heart of the old town. The guest rooms are tidily furnished in brisk modern style with air-conditioning. Rooms over-looking the square cost a few euros extra. €110.

Hotel Playa Esperanza

Avda S'Albufera 4, Port d'Alcúdia ☎971 890568, ⓦwww.esperanzahoteles .com. Luxurious, well-conceived four-star hotel with every facil-ity, including outdoor swimming pools and gymnasia. Over three hundred balconied bedrooms in a large bright-white block that backs straight onto the beach about 4km south of Port d'Alcúdia's marina. Closed Nov to Jan. €100.

Hotel Son Sant Jordi

c/Sant Jordi 29, Pollença ☎971 530389, ⓦwww.sonsantjordi.com.

This well-appointed hotel occu-pies an attractively converted old stone merchant's house in the centre of Pollença. The guest rooms are decorated in an attractive modern style in keeping with their surroundings. All rooms have a/c, satellite TV, minibar and safe, and there's a large garden out back with a sizeable pool. €140.

Hotel-residencia Sis Pins

Passeig Anglada Camarasa 77, Port de Pollença ☎971 867050, ⓕ971 866264. Medium-sized, three-star hotel occupying a handsome whitewashed and balconied villa on the pedestrianized part of the waterfront. Closed Nov–March. €125.

Monestir de Nostra Senyora de Lluc

Lluc ☎971 871525, ⓔinfo@lluc.net. At Lluc monastery, room rental is highly organized, with simple, self-contained apartment-cells and apartments. In summer, phone ahead if you want to be sure of space, at other times simply book at the monastery's information office on arrival. There's an 11pm curfew, except for the apartments, which have their own separate entrance. €15 per person.

Posada de Lluc

c/Roser Vell 11, Pollença ☎971 53 52 200, ⓦwww.posadalluc.com. This small and very comfortable hotel occupies an attractively restored old stone town house in the centre of Pollença. The monks from Lluc monastery (see p.109) used to lodge here when they popped into town to pick up supplies and many of the original features have been kept, most notably the deep stone arches. There's a small outside pool and each of the guest rooms has been kitted out in an appropriate modern version of period style. €120.

Restaurants

Café-Bar Juma

Plaça Major 9, Pollença ☎971 535002. Good range of tasty *tapas* sold in the brisk, modern bar of the *Hotel Juma*. Rapid-fire service and reasonable prices – a standard portion of *tapas* costs about €4. The outside terrace overlooking the main square is especially enticing.

Pizzeria Roma Restaurant

Avgda Pere Mas i Reus 10, Port d'Alcúdia. No phone. This is one of the more authentically Italian of Port d'Alcúdia's many pizzerias, with a wide-ranging menu offering pizza and pasta through to crêpes (which are particularly good) and steaks. It's located just off the main drag, Carretera d'Artà, across and just up the street from the main tourist office.

Restaurant Ca'n Simo

c/Sant Jaume 1, Alcúdia ☎971 549260. Chic but eminently affordable vegetarian restaurant in the heart of Alcúdia. The outside terrace with its water fountain is a lovely spot to unwind in the heat of the midday sun.

Restaurant Cantonet

c/Monti-Sion 20, Pollença ☎971 530429. This fashionable restaurant in the centre of Pollença, just north of Plaça Major, offers top-notch international cuisine from a limited menu with main courses averaging around €20. In the summer, you can eat out on the terrace of the large church next door. Evenings only; closed Tues.

▲RESTAURANT IL GIARDINO

Restaurant Il Giardino

Plaça Major 11, Pollença ☎971 534302. One the best restaurants in Pollença, this smart bistro-style place offers a superb range of Italian dishes from about €15, all prepared with great flair and gusto.

Restaurant Ivy Garden

c/Llevant 14, Port de Pollença ☎971 866271. This outstanding restaurant, arguably the best in town, features an inventive modern menu at reasonable prices. Dishes change, but include things like fillet of salmon with pesto and lemon dressing, and duck with ginger sauce. Main courses average around €20.

Restaurant Mirador de la Victòria

Beside the Santuari de la Victòria, near Alcúdia ☎971 547173. Laid-back, informal restaurant occupying a magnificent location with

▲RESTAURANT MIRADOR DE LA VICTÒRIA

modern decor and attentive service, is renowned for the quality of its seafood – though the main courses tend towards the minimal. Prices are a bit above the average, but nothing too excessive and well worth it for the romantic seashore setting out on the pier. It's a very popular spot, so reservations are well-nigh essential.

Shopping

Alcúdia market

Alcúdia. Tues & Sun from 8am. Fantastically popular open-air market, whose stalls sprawl over the east side of the town centre from Plaça Carles V to the main square, Plaça Constitució. Everything is here from the worst of tourist tat to designer clothes and fresh fruit and veg.

sweeping sea views from its expansive terrace. The food is first-rate too; guinea fowl and chicken are two specialities. Very reasonable prices; closed Mon.

Restaurant Sa Plaça

Plaça Constitució 1, Alcúdia ☎971 546278. This smart little bistro, beside the busy main street and with a pleasant pavement terrace, serves a tasty range of traditional Mallorcan dishes; main courses average around €10.

Restaurant Stay

Moll Nou jetty s/n, Port de Pollença ☎971 864013. This long-established restaurant, with its crisp

Bennassar Galleries

Plaça Major 6, Pollença ☎971 533514. Thurs–Sat 10am–1pm & 5–9pm & Sun 11am–1.30pm. Pollença has established something of a reputation for its fine-art galleries and this is perhaps the most inventive, featuring contemporary artists of various skills and techniques.

Ensenat

c/ Alcúdia 11, Pollença. Mon–Fri 10am–1.30pm & 5–7.30pm, Sat 10am–1pm. Excellent wine and speciality food shop stocked with all things *Mallorquín*, from hams and sausages to olives and almonds.

Southern Mallorca

Southern Mallorca mostly consists of the island's central plain, Es Pla, a fertile tract bounded by the Serres de Llevant, the hilly range that shadows the east coast. Before the tourist boom of the 1960s, when the developers bypassed the plain to focus on the coast, Es Pla largely defined Mallorca. The majority of the island's inhabitants lived here and it produced enough food to meet almost every domestic requirement, and even today this is where you can still get the full flavour of an older, agricultural Mallorca, whose softly hued landscapes are patterned with country towns of low, whitewashed houses. Obvious targets include Sineu, which has a particularly imposing parish church, and Petra, with its clutch of sights celebrating the life of the eighteenth-century Franciscan monk and explorer Junípero Serra. Other places worth searching out are the Gordiola Glassworks, Els Calderers, a country house illustrating *hacienda* life in the nineteenth century, and the monastery perched on the summit of Puig Randa. In the Serres de Llevant, aim for Artà's hilltop shrine, the prehistoric ruins of Ses Paisses and the medieval castle at Capdepera.

Most of the picturesque coves and tiny fishing villages of the east coast have been swallowed up within a string of mega-resorts, but three have managed to retain much of their original charm: Cala Rajada, a lively holiday spot bordered by fine beaches and a beautiful pine-shrouded coastline, Cala Figuera, which surrounds a lovely, steep-sided cove, and Porto Petro. Different again are the old and amenable port of Porto Cristo

Transport and accommodation

Direct buses link Palma with almost every resort and town in southern Mallorca, but services between the towns of Es Pla are virtually nonexistent, while those along the coast are patchy. Broadly speaking, you can manage to get a bus to almost anywhere from Manacor, as well as between Cala Rajada, Artà and Cala Millor in the north, and between Cala d'Or, Cala Figuera and Colònia de Sant Jordi in the south. The train line from Palma is also useful, linking the capital with Inca, Sineu, Petra, Manacor and Sa Pobla. Elsewhere, you'll be struggling without a car.

Given the difficulty of finding a room on spec in the coastal package resorts and the limited extent of accommodation in the interior, advance reservations are a good idea – and pretty much essential in the height of the season. In addition, three of the region's former monasteries offer simple, inexpensive lodgings, and usually have space at any time of year (see p.145–6).

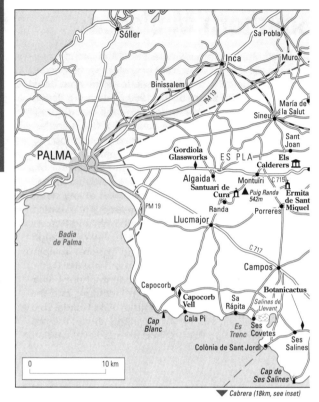

▼ Cabrera (18km, see inset)

and tiny Cala Mondragó, where a slice of coast has been belatedly protected by the creation of a park. The east coast also holds the cave systems of Coves d'Artà and Coves del Drac, famous for their dramatic stalactites and stalagmites. On the south coast, the hills and coves give way to sparse flatlands and the only star turn is the port-cum-resort of Colònia de Sant Jordi, from where boat trips leave for the scrubby remoteness of fauna-rich Cabrera island.

The Gordiola Glassworks

Ctra Palma–Manacor, km 19.
June–Sept Mon–Sat 9am–8pm, Sun 9am–1.30pm; Oct–May Mon–Sat

9am–7pm, Sun 9am–1.30pm; free. Don't be put off by C'an Gordiola, the ugly castle-like building dating from the 1960s, or by the herd of tourist coaches parked outside. Inside, you can watch highly skilled glassblowers in action, practising their precise art in a gloomy hall designed to resemble a medieval church and illuminated by glowing furnaces. Perhaps inevitably, this is all part of a public relations exercise intended to push you towards the adjacent gift shops, which hold a massive assortment of glass and ceramic items.

The gift shops are one thing, but the museum, on the top floor, is quite another. The

owners of the glassworks, the Gordiola family, have been in business in Mallorca since the early eighteenth century and they have accumulated an extraordinary collection of glassware, now displayed in fifty-odd cabinets. Of the pieces on display, some of the most interesting are the earliest Gordiola work, green-coloured jugs of a frothy consistency, where both the shade and the trapped air bubbles were unwanted – only later did improved technology allow for colour clarification and the removal of the last air bubbles. Amongst later work, kitchen- and tableware predominate – bottles, vases, jugs and

▲ GORDIOLA GLASSWORKS

glasses in a variety of shades, of which green remains the most distinctive. The Gordiola pieces are, however, but a fraction of the collection, with other cabinets featuring pieces from every corner of the globe.

Algaida and Puig Randa

Algaida is typical of the small agricultural towns that sprinkle Mallorca's central plain – low, whitewashed houses fanning out from an old Gothic-Baroque church. There's nothing remarkable about the place, but if you're travelling the C715 you'll need to pass through here to reach the 5km-long byroad that clambers to the top of Puig Randa, at 542 metres the highest of a slim band of hills lying to the north of Llucmajor.

The top of Puig Randa is flat enough to accommodate a substantial walled complex, the Santuari de Nostra Senyora de Cura (Hermitage of Our Lady

▼SANTUARI DE NOSTRA SENYORA DE CURA

of Cura). Entry is through a seventeenth-century portal, but most of the buildings beyond are plain and modern, the work of the present incumbents, Franciscan monks who arrived in 1913 after the site had lain abandoned for decades. The oldest surviving building is the quaintly gabled chapel, a homely and familiar affair partly dating from the 1660s, but you'll soon be moving on to either the terrace café, which offers average food and superb views, or the information office, where you can fix yourself up with a room.

There are also two other, less significant sanctuaries on the lower slopes of Puig Randa. Heading back down the hill, it's a couple of kilometres to the easily missable sharp left turn for the Santuari de Sant Honorat, which comprises a tiny church and a few conventual buildings of medieval provenance.

Back on the main summit road, a further 1.2km down the hill, is the more appealing third and final monastery, the Santuari de Gràcia, which is approached through a signposted gateway on the left. Founded in the fifteenth century, the whitewashed walls of this tiny sanctuary are tucked underneath a severe cliff face, which throngs with nesting birds, and there are panoramic view of Es Pla's rolling farmland.

Montuïri

Montuïri is a gentle sweep of pastel-shaded stone houses on a low hill immediately north of the main C715. In the heart of the town, it's worth taking a peek at the largely Gothic church of Sant Bartomeu, an imposing pile plonked next to the small main square and the proud possessor of several handsome Baroque altarpieces.

The next place of interest on the C715 east of Montuïri is the fascinating old country house of Els Calderers (see p.131), but the town is also a convenient starting point for the short detour north along country roads to Sineu and Petra (see below). In addition, Montuïri is close to the old hilltop monastery of Ermita de Sant Miquel, signposted north off the C715 just east of the town; this is now the location of a café-restaurant with smashing views over the central plain.

Sineu

Sineu is undoubtedly the most interesting of the ancient agricultural towns of the central plain. Glued to a hill at the geographical centre of the island, the town had obvious strategic advantages for the independent kings of fourteenth-century Mallorca. Jaume II built a royal palace here; his asthmatic successor Sancho came to take the upland air; and the last of the dynasty, Jaume III, slept in Sineu the night before he was defeated and killed at the battle of Llucmajor by Pedro of Aragón.

The new Aragonese monarchs had no need of the Sineu palace, which disappeared long ago, but former pretensions survive in the massive stone facade of Nostra Senyora de los Angeles, the grandest parish church on the island. Built in the thirteenth century, the church was extensively remodelled three hundred years later, but the majestic simplicity of the original Gothic design is still plain to see – though it's in a poor state of repair. At the side, a

▲SINEU

single-span arch connects with the colossal free-standing bell tower, and at the front, at the top of the steps, a big, modern and aggressive statue of a winged lion – the emblem of the town's patron, St Mark – stands guard, courtesy of Franco's cronies.

Beside the church is the unassuming main square, Sa Plaça, where you'll find a couple of traditional Mallorcan bar-restaurants, which are packed to the gunnels on Wednesdays, when the town fizzes with Mallorca's biggest fresh produce and livestock markets.

Petra

Nothing very exciting happens in Petra but it was the birthplace of Junípero Serra, the eighteenth-century Franciscan friar who played an important role in the settlement of Spanish

▲JUNÍPERO SERRA HOUSE, PETRA

North America. Serra's missionary endeavours began in 1749 when he landed at Veracruz on the Gulf of Mexico. For eighteen years Serra thrashed around the remoter parts of Mexico until, entirely by chance, political machinations back in Europe saved him from obscurity. In 1768, Carlos III claimed the west coast of the North American continent for Spain and, to substantiate his claim, dispatched a small expeditionary force of soldiers and monks north; Serra led the priests. The walk from Mexico City to California was pretty daunting, but almost all the force survived to reach the Pacific Ocean somewhere near the present US–Mexico border in early 1769. Over the next decade, Serra and his small party of priests set about converting the Native Americans of coastal California to the Catholic faith, and established a string of nine missions along the Pacific coast, including San Diego, Los Angeles and San Francisco. Pope John Paul II beatified Serra in 1988.

Petra makes a reasonable hand of its connection with Serra. In the upper part of town, on c/Major, is the chunky church of Sant Bernat, beside which – down a narrow side street – lies a modest sequence of majolica panels honouring Serra's life and missionary work. This simple tribute is backed up by a self-effacing museum (no fixed opening hours) in a pleasant old house at the end of this same side street, with several rooms devoted to Serra's cult. Three doors up the street, at no. 6, is the humble whitewashed stone and brick house where he was born. The museum and house are sometimes locked, but there should be instructions posted outside explaining how to contact the custodian.

Ermita de Nostra Senyora de Bonany

The hilltop Ermita de Nostra Senyora de Bonany, some 5km southwest of Petra, offers extensive views over Es Pla. To get there, take the Felanitx road out of Petra and look out for the sign on the edge of the village. The monastery is at the end of a bumpy, four-kilometre country lane, and takes its name from events in 1609 when desperate locals gathered here at the chapel to pray for rain. Shortly afterwards, the drought broke and the ensuing harvest was a good one – hence *bon any* ("good year"). The prettiest feature of the complex is the chapel, which is approached along an avenue of cypress and palm trees and comes complete with a rose window, twin towers and a little cupola. The monastery's conspicuous stone cross was erected in honour of Junípero Serra, who left here bound for the Americas in 1749. There are also five simple double rooms for rent here (see p.145).

Els Calderers

Daily: April–Sept 10am–6pm; Oct–March 10am–5pm; €7. Dating mostly from the eighteenth century, Els Calderers is a charming country house that bears witness to the wealth and influence once enjoyed by the island's landed gentry – in this case the Veri family. It's tucked away at the end of a country lane 2km north of – and clearly signposted from – the C715.

The house was the focus of a large estate which produced a mixed bag of agricultural produce: the main cash crop was originally grapes, though this changed in the 1870s when phylloxera, a greenfly-like aphid, destroyed Mallorca's (and most of Europe's) vineyards. The Veris switched to cereals, and at the beginning of the twentieth century were at the forefront of efforts to modernize Mallorcan agriculture. The entrance to the house, flanked by a pair of crumpled-looking lions, leads to a sequence of handsome rooms surrounding a cool courtyard. All are kitted out with antique furniture, *objets d'art* and family portraits, and each has a clearly defined function, from the dainty music room to the hunting room, with assorted stuffed animal heads, and the master's office, with big armchairs and a much-polished desk. You can also see the family's tiny chapel and there's more religious material upstairs in the assorted prints that line the walls. Attached to, but separate from, the family house are the living quarters of the *amo* (farm manager), the barn and the farmworkers' kitchen and eating area. To complete your visit, take a stroll round the animal pens, which hold breeds traditionally used on Mallorcan farms, and pop into the café, where they serve traditional island snacks – the *pa amb oli* (bread rubbed with olive oil) with ham and cheese is delicious.

Manacor

Manacor declares its business long before you arrive, with vast roadside hoardings promoting its furniture, wrought-iron and artificial pearl factories. On the strength of these, the city has become Mallorca's second urban centre, much smaller than Palma, but large enough to have spawned sprawling suburbs on all sides. Fortunately, the historic centre has been attractively restored and this is where you should head for. The most impressive building is the Església Nostra Senyora Verge dels Dolors, the principal church, whose left transept holds an idiosyncratic full-sized polychrome crucified Christ wearing a skirt.

While you're here, be sure to try the local speciality – spicy pork sausage made from the Mallorcan black pig (*sobrasada de cerdo negro*). One good place to sample it is the *Palau Café*, across from the church at Plaça Rector Rubí 8 (closed Sun).

Artà

The top end of the Serres de Llevant range bunches to fill out Mallorca's eastern corner, providing a dramatic backdrop to Artà, an ancient hill town of sun-bleached roofs clustered beneath a castellated chapel-shrine. It's a delightful scene, though at close quarters the town is something of an anticlimax with the cobweb of cramped and twisted alleys not quite matching the setting. That said, the ten-minute trek up to the Santuari de Sant Salvador, the panoramic shrine at the top of Artà, is a must. It's almost impossible to get lost – just keep going upwards: follow c/Ciutat as it slices across the edge of Plaça Conqueridor, and then head straight on up to Plaça Espanya, a leafy little piazza that is home to the town hall. Beyond, a short stroll through streets of gently decaying mansions brings you to the gargantuan parish church of Sant Salvador. From this unremarkable pile, steep stone steps and cypress trees lead up the Via Crucis (Way of the Cross) to the *santuari*, which, in its present form,

dates from the early nineteenth century, though the hilltop has been a place of pilgrimage for much longer. The interior of the present chapel is hardly awe-inspiring – the paintings are mediocre and the curious statue of Jesus behind the altar has him smiling as if he has lost his marbles – but the views are exquisite, with the picturesque town below and Es Pla stretching away to distant hills.

Ses Paisses

April–Sept Mon–Sat 9.30am–1pm & 4–7pm; Oct–March Mon–Fri 9am–1pm & 2–5pm; €1.50. Tucked away in a grove of olive, carob and holm-oak trees, the elegiacally rustic prehistoric remains of the Talayotic village of Ses Paisses are about 1km south of Artà. To get there, walk to the bottom of c/Ciutat, turn left along the main through-road and watch for the signposted and well-surfaced country lane on the right. A clear footpath explores every nook and cranny of the site, and its numbered markers are thoroughly explained in the English-language guidebook available at the entrance (€1.80).

▼ ARTÀ

The village is entered through a monolithic gateway, whose heavyweight jambs and lintel interrupt the Cyclopean walls that still encircle the site. These outer remains date from the second phase of the Talayotic culture (c.1000–800 BC), when the emphasis was on consolidation and defence; in places, the walls still stand at their original size, around 3.5m high and 3m thick. Beside the gate, there's also a modern plinth erected in honour of Miquel Llobera, a local writer who penned romantic verses about the place.

Beyond the gateway, the central talayot is from the first Talayotic phase (c.1300–1000 BC), its shattered ruins flanked by the foundations of several rooms of later date and uncertain purpose. Experts believe the horseshoe-shaped room was used, at least towards the end of the Talayotic period, for cremations, whilst the three rectangular rooms were probably living quarters. In the rooms, archeologists discovered various items such as iron objects and ceramics imported from elsewhere in the Mediterranean. Some of them were perhaps brought back from the Punic Wars (264–146 BC) by mercenaries – the skills of Balearic stone-slingers were highly prized by the Carthaginians, and it's known that several hundred accompanied Hannibal and his elephants over the Alps in 218 BC.

The Ermita de Betlem

The Ermita de Betlem, hidden in the hills 10km northwest of Artà, is a remote and minuscule hermitage founded in 1805. The road to the *ermita* begins immediately to the west of Artà's Plaça Espanya, but the start is poorly signed and tricky to find. The road's rough surface and snaking course also make for a difficult drive, so it's far better to walk – reckon on five or six hours for the return trip from Artà to the *ermita* and back.

The first portion is an easy stroll up along the wooded valley of the Torrent d'es Cocones, but then – after about 3km – the road squeezes through the narrowest of defiles, with the hills rising steeply on either side. Beyond, the road begins to climb into the foothills of the Serra de Llevant (here classified as the Massís d'Artà) until, some 3km after the defile, a signposted left turn signals the start of the strenuous part of the journey. Here, the track wriggles for 4km up the steep hillside before finally reaching the *ermita*.

The buildings, which date from the hermitage's foundation, are unassuming – although, if you've come this far, you'll undoubtedly want to peep into the tiny church, where the walls are decorated with crude religious frescoes. The hermitage doesn't offer accommodation or food, just picnic tables, but the views over the Badia d'Alcúdia are magnificent.

Cala Rajada

Awash with cafés, bars and hotels, vibrant Cala Rajada lies on the southerly side of a stubby headland in the northeast corner of Mallorca. The resort was once a fishing village, but there's little evidence of this today, and the harbour is now packed with cruise and pleasure boats. Otherwise, the pocket-sized centre is no more than an unassuming patchwork of low-rise modern buildings, but it's all very neat and trim and there's compensation nearby in the wild and rocky coastline, where pine-clad hills shelter a series of delightful beaches.

From the harbour, walkways extend along the headland's south coast. To the southwest, past the busiest part of town, it takes about ten to fifteen minutes to stroll round to Platja Son Moll, a slender arc of sand overlooked by Goliath-like hotels. More rewarding is the ten-minute stroll east from the harbour to Cala Gat, a narrow cove beach tucked tight up against the steep, wooded coastline. The beach is far from undiscovered – there's a beach bar and at times it gets decidedly crowded – but it's an attractive spot all the same.

Up above the footpath to Cala Gat you can glimpse the gardens of the Palau Joan March, a lavish mansion built in 1916 for the eponymous tobacco baron (see p.56). Beyond the gardens,

▼CALA AGULLA BEACH, CALA RAJADA

continuing east along c/Elíonor Servera, the road twists steeply up through the pine woods to reach, after about 1km, the bony headlands and lighthouse of the Cap de Capdepera, Mallorca's most easterly point.

On the northern side of Cala Rajada, c/L'Agulla crosses the promontory to hit the north coast at Platja Cala Agulla. The approach road, some 2km of tourist tackiness, is of little appeal, but the beach, a vast curve of bright golden sand, is big enough to accommodate hundreds of bronzing pectorals with plenty of space to spare. The further you walk – and there are signed and shaded footpaths through the pine woods to assist you – the more isolation you'll get.

Capdepera

Spied across the valley from the west or south, the crenellated walls dominating Capdepera, a tiny village 8km east of Artà and 3km west of Cala Rajada, look too pristine to be true. Yet the triangular fortifications are genuine enough, built in the fourteenth century by the Mallorcan king Sancho to protect the coast from pirates. The village, snuggled below the walls, contains a pleasant medley of old houses, its slender main square, Plaça de L'Orient, acting as a prelude to the steep steps up to the Castell de Capdepera (daily: April–Oct 9am–8pm; Nov–March 9am–5pm; €2). The steps are the most pleasant way to reach the castle, but you can also follow the signs and drive up narrow c/Major. Flowering cactuses give the fortress a special allure in late May and June, but it's a beguiling place at any time, with over 400m of walls equipped with a parapet

▲CAPDAPERA

walkway and sheltering neat terraced gardens. At the top of the fortress, Nostra Senyora de la Esperança (Our Lady of Good Hope) is the quaintest of Gothic churches: its aisle-less, vaulted frame is furnished with outside steps leading up, behind the bell gable, to a flat roof, from where the views are simply superb.

The Coves d'Artà

Guided tours of the caves run every half-hour daily: May–Oct 10am–7pm; Nov–April 10am–5pm; €8. The succession of coves, caves and beaches notching the Mallorcan seashore between Cala Rajada and Cala Millor begins promisingly with the memorable Coves d'Artà (often signposted in Castilian as "Cuevas de Artà"), reached along the first turning off the main coastal road (the PM404) south of Capdepera.

This is the pick of the numerous cave systems of eastern Mallorca, its sequence of cavernous chambers, studded with stalagmites and stalactites, extending 450m into the rock face. Artificial lighting exaggerates the bizarre shapes of the caverns and their accretions, especially in the Hall of Flags, where stalactites up to 50m long hang in the shape of partly

unfurled flags. Exiting the caves, you're greeted with a stunning view, courtesy of a majestic stairway straight out of a horror movie which leads down from the yawning hole, beckoning like the mouth of hell high in the cliffs above the bay.

The caves have had a chequered history. During the Reconquista, a thousand Moorish refugees from Artà were literally smoked out of the caves to be slaughtered by Catalan soldiers waiting outside. In the nineteenth century, touring the caves for their scientific interest became fashionable amongst the rich and famous – Jules Verne was particularly impressed – and visits now feature prominently on many a package-tour itinerary. Allow about an hour for the visit – more if there's a queue, as there sometimes is.

Cala Millor

The well-heeled villas of Costa dels Pins comprise the most northerly and prosperous portion of a gigantic resort conurbation centred on Cala Bona and Cala Millor. This is development gone quite mad, a swathe of apartment buildings, sky-rise hotels and villa-villages overwhelming the contours of the coast as far as the eye can see. The only redeeming feature – and the reason for all this frantic construction in the first place – is the beach, a magnificent two-kilometre stretch of sand fringed by what remains of the old pine woods. A headland away there are yet more acres of concrete and glass at Sa Coma and S'Illot. To avoid this visual assault, stay on the main coastal road – the PM404 – which runs just inland from the resorts, cutting a rustic route through vineyards and almond groves before reaching the multicoloured billboards which announce the cave systems of Porto Cristo.

Porto Cristo

Although Porto Cristo prospered in the early days of the tourist boom, sprouting a string of hotels and *hostals*, it's fared badly since mega-resorts such as Cala Millor and Cala d'Or were constructed nearby. Don't be deceived by the jam of tourist buses clogging the town's streets on their way to the nearby Coves del Drac (see below) – few of their occupants will actually be staying here. Consequently, this is one of the very few places on the east coast where you're likely to find a room on spec in July and August, and it's not too bad a spot to spend a night either, having benefited from a recent revamp. It's also got a beach, a small sliver of sand, which is good enough for sunbathing, though the swimming is poor; the beach is tucked inside the harbour, a narrow V-shaped channel entered between a pair of rocky promontories that is one of the most sheltered ports on Mallorca's east coast.

Porto Cristo's origins are uncertain, but it was definitely in existence by the thirteenth century, when it served as the fishing harbour and seaport of the inland town of Manacor. Nothing remains of the medieval settlement, however, and today the centre, which climbs the hill behind the harbour, consists of high-sided terraced buildings mostly dating from the late nineteenth and early twentieth centuries. In August 1936, Porto Cristo was the site of a Republican landing to try to capture the island from Franco's Falangists. The campaign was a fiasco: the Republicans disembarked over seven thousand men and quickly established a long and deep bridgehead, but their commanders, completely surprised by their initial success, quite literally didn't know what to do next. The Nationalists did: they counterattacked and, supported by the Italian air force, soon had the Republicans dashing back to the coast. Barcelona radio put on a brave face, announcing, "The heroic Catalan columns have returned from Mallorca after a magnificent action. Not a single man suffered from the effects of the embarkation."

Coves del Drac

Hourly guided tours daily: April–Oct 10am–5pm; Nov–March 10.30am–2pm; €7.50. Porto Cristo's pride and joy, the Coves del Drac (often signposted in Castilian "Cuevas del Drach"), is located across the Es Rivet river, about fifteen minutes' walk south of the town centre along the coastal road. Locals had known of the "Dragon's Caves" for hundreds of years, but it was the Austrian archduke Ludwig Salvator (see p.94) who recruited French geologists to explore and map them in 1896. The French

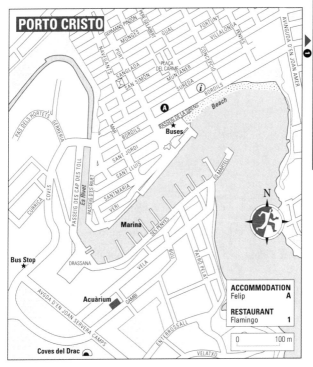

discovered four huge chambers that penetrated the coast's limestone cliffs for a distance of around 2km. In the last cavern they found one of the largest subterranean lakes in the world, some 177m long, 40m wide and 30m deep.

Thoroughly commercialized, the present complex accommodates a giant car park, ticket office and restaurant, behind which lurk the gardens that lead to the flight of steps down to the caves. You may come to know each step well, as you can wait in line for ages, especially at the weekend.

Inside, the myriad concretions of calcium carbonate, formed by the dissolution of the soft limestone by rainwater, are shrewdly illuminated. Shunting you

through the hour-long, multi-lingual tour, the guides invite you to gawp and gush at formations such as "the Buddha" and "the Pagoda", as well as magnificent icicle-like stalactites, some of which are snowy white, others picking up hints of orange and red from the rocks they hang off. The *tour de force* is the larger of the two subterranean lakes, whose translucent waters flicker with reflected colours, the effects enhanced by a small group of musicians drifting by in boats; performances usually begin on the hour.

From the cave complex, it's a short walk across the car park to the well-stocked Acuàrium (Aquarium; daily: April–Sept 11am–6pm; Oct–March 11am–3pm; €5).

Coves d'es Hams

Guided tours every half-hour daily: April–Oct 10am–6pm; Nov–March 10.30am–5pm; €9.50. The Coves d'es Hams (or "Cuevas del Hams" in Castilian), situated 2km west of Porto Cristo on the road to Manacor, are not nearly as well known as their subterranean neighbour, the Coves del Drac, but a visit follows the same format. Guides escort their charges through a sequence of caverns lit to emphasize the beauty of the accumulated stalagmites, and stalactites and the whole caboodle culminates with musicians playing from boats on an underground lake.

Porto Colom

Porto Colom straggles round a long and irregular bay some 20km south of Porto Cristo. Originally a fishing village supplying the needs of the neighbouring town of Felanitx, the port boomed throughout most of the nineteenth century from the export trade in wine to France. The good times, however, came to an abrupt end when phylloxera wiped out the island's vines in the 1870s. The villagers returned to fishing, which still makes up a significant part of the local economy: the boats they use, as well as some old boat sheds, litter the kilometre-long quay on the southwest side of the bay.

The quayside, along with the modest settlement immediately behind it, constitutes the heart of the present village and although there's little to grab your attention, it's still an amiable, downbeat spot. The oldest part of the village is about 300m from the west end of the quay, round the back of the harbour, and comprises a small parcel of pastel-shaded cottages shadowing a little square. Elsewhere, the headlands overlooking the entrance to the bay house a lighthouse and an unappetizing mix of villas and hotels, while over the hill behind the village (about 1km to the south) is Cala Marçal, a crowded, shadeless wedge of sand overlooked by the concrete flanks of the eponymous hotel.

Felanitx

Small-town Felanitx is an industrious place, producing wine, ceramics and pearls, and although it's hardly beautiful, it does have more than a modicum of charm, its tangle of narrow streets lined by handsome old houses mostly dating from the eighteenth and nineteenth centuries. The finest building is the church of Sant Miquel, whose honey-gold, Baroque facade adds a touch of elegance to the largely modern main square, Plaça Constitució. A plaque on the church recalls the worst disaster to hit the town since the days of pirate attack, when a wall collapsed killing over four hundred people on their way from church. There are no other sights as such, but strolling the old streets and alleys is an agreeable way to pass the odd hour; the best time to visit is on Sunday morning, when the main square is given over to a lively fresh produce and craft market. In particular, look out for the capers (Catalan *tapèras*; Castilian *alcaparras*), produced locally and sold by size; the smallest are the most flavourful, either as nonpareilles (up to 7mm) or surfines (7–8mm).

The Santuari de Sant Salvador

Within easy striking distance of Felanitx is one of the more scenic portions of the band of hills known as the Serres de Llevant. The best approach is to head east along the road to Porto Colom for about 2km, then take the signposted, four-kilometre tarmac byroad that wriggles up the mountain to the Santuari de Sant Salvador, recognizable from miles around by its conspicuous stone cross and enormous statue of Christ. Long an important place of pilgrimage, the monastery occupies a splendid position near the summit of the highest mountain in these parts, the 510-metre Puig de Sant Salvador, with sumptuous views out over the east coast.

The sanctuary was founded in the mid-fourteenth century, but the original buildings were razed by raiding pirates and most of today's complex is Baroque. The heavy gatehouse is its most conspicuous feature while, inside the compound, the eighteenth-century church shelters a much-venerated image of the Virgin Mary. This was the last of Mallorca's monasteries to lose its monks – the last ones moved out in the early 1990s – and it now rents out fourteen rudimentary guest rooms (see p.146).

The Castell de Santueri

The custodians at the Santuari de Sant Salvador should be able to point you towards the footpath to the Castell de Santueri, about 4km away across the hills to the south. The route is fairly easy to follow and the going isn't difficult, although it's still advisable to have a walking map and stout shoes. The path meanders through a pretty landscape of dry stone walls, flowering shrubs and copses of almond and carob trees, bringing you to the castle

after about an hour and a half. Glued to a rocky hilltop, the battered ramparts date from the fourteenth century, though the first fastness here was built by the Moors. Getting inside the ruins is pot luck: sometimes you can (in which case a small entry fee is levied at the main gate), and sometimes you can't. If you don't fancy the walk, you can drive to the castle along a five-kilometre country lane, signed off the Santanyí road about 2km south of Felanitx.

Cala d'Or

South along the coast from Porto Colom, the pretty little fishing villages that once studded the quiet coves as far as Porto Petro have been blasted by development. The interconnected resorts that now stand in their place are a largely indistinguishable strip of whitewashed, low-rise villas, hotels, restaurants and bars, all designed in a sort of *pueblo* style. Confusingly, this long string of resorts is now usually lumped together under the title Cala d'Or, though technically this name in fact refers to one particular cove. To be fair, the pseudo-Andalusian style of the new resorts blends well with the ritzy *haciendas* left by a previous generation of sun-seekers. The latter are largely concentrated on the humpy little headland which separates the "real" Cala d'Or from its northerly neighbour, Cala Gran. These two fetching little coves, tucked between the cliffs and edged by narrow golden beaches, are the highlights of the area. The beaches are jam-packed throughout the season, but the swimming is perfect and the wooded coastline here is far preferable to the more concentrated development all around.

Porto Petro

Appealing Porto Petro rambles round a twin-pronged cove a couple of kilometres south of Cala Gran. In the last few years, it's been swallowed by the Cala d'Or conurbation, but there's no beach here so development has been restrained. The old fishing harbour has been turned into a marina, immaculate villas dot the gentle wooded hillsides and the old centre of the village, a tiny cluster of whitewashed houses perched on the headland above the marina, has survived in good order. The main activity is to take a boat trip or promenade round the crystal-watered cove.

The Mondragó Parc Natural

It may be rather late in the day, but the Balearic government has finally stepped in to protect a small slice of the east coast by creating the Mondragó Parc Natural, whose diverse terrain incorporates patches of wetland, farmland, beach, pine and scrub just to the south of Porto Petro. The park is still relatively undeveloped and the road signs are a bit confusing, but there are two car parks to aim for, both signposted from the C717 between Porto Petro and Santanyí. The better target is the Fonts de N'Alis car park, 100m from the tiny resort of Cala Mondragó; the other car park, S'Amarador, is on the low-lying headland to the east of the cove. The park is latticed with footpaths and country lanes, but currently the maps provided by the visitor centre (☎971 181022) at the Fonts de N'Alis car park are really rather poor. Fortunately, three easy hiking trails have been marked out, all are simple loops, two of forty minutes, one of twenty, and the billboard map

beside the visitor centre is a reliable reference.

Cala Mondragó

Cala Mondragó is one of Mallorca's prettiest resorts. There was some development here before the creation of Mondragó Parc Natural in 1990, but it's all very low key and barely disturbs the cove's beauty, with low, pine-clad cliffs framing a pair of sandy beaches beside crystal-clear waters. Predictably, the cove's "unspoilt" reputation and safe bathing acts as a magnet for sun-lovers from miles around, but you can escape the crowds by staying the night (if there's space) at either of two beachside *hostals*.

Santanyí

The crossroads town of Santanyí was once an important medieval stronghold guarding the island's southeastern approaches. Turkish and Berber pirates ransacked the place on several occasions, but one of the old town gates, Sa Porta, has survived along with the occasional chunk of masonry from the old city walls. Otherwise, it's Santanyí's narrow alleys, squeezed between high-sided stone houses, that are the town's main appeal, not to mention the amenable pavement cafés edging the main square.

Cala Figuera and Cala Santanyí

Travelling southeast from Santanyí, a 5km-long byroad cuts a pretty, rustic route through to Cala Figuera, whose antique harbour sits beside a fjord-like inlet below the steepest of coastal cliffs. Local fishermen still land their catches and mend their nets here, but nowadays it's to the accompaniment of scores of photo-snapping tourists. Up above, the pine-covered shoreline heaves with villas, hotels and *hostals*, although the absence of high-rise buildings means the development is never overbearing. What you won't get is a beach. The nearest is 4km west at Cala Santanyí, a busy little resort with a medium-sized (and frequently crowded) beach at the end of a steep-sided, heavily wooded gulch. To get there, head back towards Santanyí for about 2km and follow the signs.

Cap de Ses Salines

Heading southwest from Santanyí, a fast and easy country road drifts through a landscape of old dry-stone walls, broken-down windmills, ochre-flecked farmhouses and straggling fields on its way towards Colònia de Sant Jordi (see below). After about 4km, you pass through tiny Es Llombards and shortly afterwards reach the turning that leads the 10km down through coastal pine woods to the light-house on Cap de Ses Salines, a bleak, brush-covered headland which is Mallorca's most southerly point. The lighthouse itself is closed to the public, but there are fine views out to sea. Thekla larks and stone curlews are often to be seen on the cape, whilst gulls, terns and shearwaters glide about offshore, benefiting from the winds which, when they're up, can make the place well-nigh intolerable.

Botanicactus

Carretera Santanyí s/n. Daily: April–Sept 9am–7pm; Oct–March 9am–5pm; €6.20. On the road to Colònia de Sant Jordi, billboards welcome you to Botanicactus, a huge botanical garden mostly devoted to indigenous and imported species of cactus. A surprise here is the artificial lake, which encourages the growth of wetland plants – a welcome splash in arid surroundings – but otherwise the place has all the atmosphere of a glorified garden centre.

Colònia de Sant Jordi

Altogether one of the most appealing of Mallorca's mid-range resorts, the wide streets and breezy avenues of Colònia de Sant Jordi pattern a substantial and irregularly shaped headland about 13km west of Santanyí. The main approach road is the Avinguda Marquès del Palmer, at the end of which – roughly in the middle of the headland – lies the principal square, the unremarkable Plaça Constitució. From here, c/Sa Solta and then Avinguda Primavera lead west to the sprawling *Hotel Marquès del Palmer*, sitting tight against the Platja d'Estanys, whose gleaming sands curve round a dune-edged cove.

South of Avinguda Primavera is the surprisingly pleasant main tourist zone, the domineering

▼COLÒNIA DE SANT JORDI HARBOUR

Southern Mallorca **PLACES**

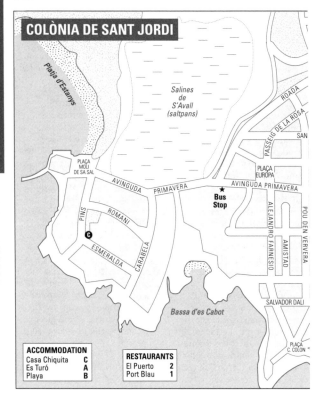

COLÒNIA DE SANT JORDI

Platja d'Estanys

Salines de S'Avall (saltpans)

ROADA

PASSEIG DE LA ROSA

SAN

PLAÇA MOLI DE SA SAL

AVINGUDA PRIMAVERA

PLAÇA EUROPA

AVINGUDA PRIMAVERA

★ Bus Stop

PINS

ROMANI

ESMERALDA

CARABELA

ALEJANDRO FARNESIO

POU DEN VERVERA

AMISTAD

SALVADOR DALI

Bassa d'es Cabot

PLAÇA C. COLON

ACCOMMODATION	
Casa Chiquita	**C**
Es Turó	**A**
Playa	**B**

RESTAURANTS	
El Puerto	**2**
Port Blau	**1**

lines of its flashy hotels broken by low-rise villas and landscaped side streets. To the north are the Salines de S'Avall, the saltpans which once provided the town with its principal source of income. East from Plaça Constitució along c/Major, and then left (north) down c/Gabriel Roca, is the old harbour, the most diverting part of town. Framed by an attractive, early twentieth-century ensemble of balconied houses, the port makes the most of a handsome, horseshoe-shaped bay. There's nothing special to look at, but it's a relaxing spot with a handful of restaurants, fishing smacks, a marina and a pocket-sized beach,

the Platja Es Port. From here, it's a five-minute walk along the footpath north round the bay onto the slender, low-lying headland that accommodates the much more extensive sands of the Platja d'es Dolç.

Es Trenc

One of Colònia de Sant Jordi's attractions is its proximity to Es Trenc, a 4km strip of sandy beach that extends as far as the eye can see. It's neither unknown, nor unspoilt, but the crowds are easily absorbed except at the highest point of high season, and development is virtually nonexistent. To drive there, head north from Colònia

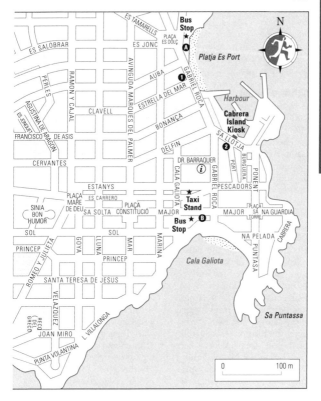

de Sant Jordi and, about 1km out of town, turn left towards Campos; then, after another 2.8km, take the signed left turn and follow the country lanes leading across the salt flats to the large car park (€4) at the east end of the beach – a total distance of around 7km. This end of the beach is far more appealing than the other, at Ses Covetes, which is splotched by improvised shacks and drinks stalls.

Salines de Llevant

The saltpans backing onto Es Trenc – the Salines de Llevant – and the surrounding farm and scrubland support a wide variety of birdlife. Residents such as marsh harriers, kestrels, spotted crakes, fan-tailed warblers and hoopoes make a visit enjoyable at any time of year, but the best time to come is in the spring when hundreds of migrants arrive from Africa. Commonly seen in the springtime are avocets, little ringed plovers, little egrets, common sandpipers, little stints, black-tailed godwits, collared pratincoles and black terns. Several footpaths lead from Es Trenc beach into the saltpans, but it's not a good area to explore on foot: the scenery is boring, it's smelly and for much of the year insects are a menace. It's much better to drive or cycle round using the maze-like network of narrow country lanes that traverse the saltpans, stopping anywhere that looks promising.

Cabrera island

Boat trips to Cabrera depart Sant Jordi harbour (April–Oct 1 daily; 8hr; €28). Advance reservations are essential with Excursions A Cabrera (☎971 649034), either by phone or in person at their harbourside kiosk. Take your own food – plus fresh fruit for the lizards – or shell out €6 for the boat company buffet (drinks are extra).

Cabrera ("Goat Island") is a bumpy, scrub-covered hunk of rock lying 18km offshore from Colònia de Sant Jordi. No more than 7km wide and 5km long, Cabrera still rustles up a long and eventful history. Pliny claimed the island to have been the birthplace of Hannibal, pirates regularly holed up here, and during the Napoleonic Wars, the Spanish stuck nine thousand French prisoners of war out here and forgot about them – two-thirds died from hunger and disease during their captivity. The island was taken over by Franco's armed forces and more recently has been designated a national park.

The day-trip from Sant Jordi begins with a sixty-minute voyage to the island followed by a speedy circumnavigation, weather permitting. On the final stretch, the boat nudges into the harbour, Es Port – a narrow finger of calm water edged by hills and equipped with a tiny jetty. Much of the island is out of bounds, but one of the walks you can make is the stiff twenty-minute hoof up to the ruins of the medieval castle, which offers stirring views over island and sea. Cabrera also teems with birdlife, but the rare, blue-underbellied Lilfords wall lizard steals the naturalist show: down by the jetty, you can tempt them out from the scrub with pieces of fruit. You can also visit Cabrera Museum (free), with displays tracing the history of the island illustrated by a ragbag of archeological finds. On the return journey, the boat makes a swim stop at the Cova Blava (Blue Grotto), a yawning cavern which reaches a height of 160m and is suffused by bluish light – hence its name.

▼CABRERA ISLAND FERRY

Llucmajor and Capocorb Vell

A middling market town, Llucmajor was long the centre of the island's shoemaking industry. It also has one historic claim to fame for it was here, just outside the old city walls, that Jaume III, the last of the independent kings of Mallorca, was defeated and killed by Pedro IV of Aragón – and centuries of Balearic neglect were to follow. Llucmajor is at the head of the byroad which leads south to Cap Blanc. About 13km along this road lies Capocorb Vell (often signposted in Castilian as "Capicorp Vey"; Mon–Wed & Fri–Sun 10am–5pm; €2), whose extensive remains date from around 1000 BC. Surrounded by arid scrubland and enclosed within a modern dry-stone wall, this prehistoric village incorporates the battered ruins of five *talayots* and 28 dwellings. A footpath weaves round the haphazard remains, but most of what you see fails to inspire and gives little idea of how the village was arranged. The most impressive features are the Cyclopean walls, which reach a height of four metres in places. To make more sense of what you see, pick up the free English leaflet at the entrance.

Accommodation

Ermita de Nostra Senyora de Bonany

Puig Bonany, Petra ☎971 561101. Some 5km southwest of Petra, this hilltop former monastery offers five simple double rooms. There's hot water (in one bathroom) and cooking facilities, but you'll have to bring your own food and bedding. To get there, take the Felanitx road out of Petra and look out for the sign on the edge of the village;

the monastery is at the end of a bumpy, four-kilometre country lane. €10 per person.

Hostal Casa Chiquita

c/Esmeralda 14, Colònia de Sant Jordi ☎971 655121, ⊛www.casachiquita .es. This smart and well-tended *hostal* occupies a rambling, *pueblo*-style modern villa in the tourist zone at the west end of Avinguda Primavera. It has a good-looking garden, with lots of exotic cactuses, and eighteen smartly decorated en-suite guest rooms. Closed mid-Oct to Feb. €115.

Hostal Ca's Bombu

c/Elíonor Servera 86, Cala Rajada ☎971 563203, ⊛www.casbombu .com. This eminently appealing, family-run, two-star *hostal* has fifty unpretentious rooms with substantial wooden furniture. There's a swimming pool too, plus a first-rate terrace restaurant overlooking the water. Breakfast included. A snip at €40.

Hostal Es Turó

c/Gabriel Roca 38, Colònia de Sant Jordi ☎971 655057. Unassuming, recently revamped one-star *hostal* in a solid three-storey building plonked right on Es Port beach. There's a rooftop swimming pool and eighteen guest rooms – those at the back look out over the beach. Closed Nov–March. €50.

Hostal Playa

c/Major 25, Colònia de Sant Jordi ☎ & ☎971 655256. About five minutes' walk from the harbour, this cosy and well-cared-for little *hostal* has folksy bygones in its public areas and eight spotless en-suite rooms. Breakfast is served on a pretty patio terrace with views out along the seashore. €60.

Hotel Felip

c/Bordils 61, Porto Cristo ☎971 820750, ⊛www.thbhotels.com. This three-star hotel has a great location, in a big old balconied building overlooking the town beach. The interior has been revamped in modern style and the rooms are neat and trim – ask for a harbour view. Closed Oct–Dec. €100.

Hotel Leon de Sineu

c/Bous 129, Sineu ☎971 520211, ⊛www.hotel-leondesineu.com. Set in a beautifully refurbished old mansion, this excellent hotel kicks off in style with a spacious and elegant wood-beamed foyer. Beyond, each of the bedrooms is tastefully furnished in an uncluttered antique style and at the back the well-tended garden has an outdoor pool and a breakfast terrace. The hotel is located five minutes' stroll from the main square, Sa Plaça – walk down the hill from the square, turn first right and keep going. €120.

Hotel Ses Rotges

c/Rafael Blanes 21, Cala Rajada ☎971 563108, ⊛www.sesrotges.com. Delightful three-star establishment in an elegantly restored antique villa just out of earshot of the main square. Each of the 24 guest rooms has a beamed ceiling and a tiled floor. The hotel restaurant is the classiest in town (see below). Closed Nov–March. €90.

Santuari de Nostra Senyora de Cura

Puig Randa, Algaida ☎971 120260. This one-time monastery, on top of Puig Randa near Algaida, offers simple rooms in its guest quarters, a self-contained, modern block opposite the chapel. €15 per person.

Santuari de Sant Salvador

Puig de Sant Salvador ☎971 827282. Perched on top of the 510-metre Puig de Sant Salvador, some six kilometres east of Felanitx, this former monastery has fourteen spartan guest rooms sleeping between two and nine people. Ten of the rooms have shared bathrooms, four are en suite. There's hot water and a café-restaurant (it's best to call ahead to confirm opening hours) and bedding is provided. Shared bathroom €8 per person, en suite €10 per person.

Restaurants

Café Parisien

c/Ciutat 18, Artà ☎971 835440. Closed Sun lunch. Chic little bistro with an outside terrace and slick modern decor serving tasty *tapas* and salads at reasonable prices. C/Ciutat is Artà's short main street.

Celler Es Grop

c/Major 18, Sineu ☎971 520187. Closed Sun & Mon eve. Traditional bar-restaurant, whose cavernous interior doubles as a wine vault – hence the enormous wooden barrels. Serves hearty, inexpensive snacks from as little as €5, €20 for a full meal. Packed to the gunnels on Wednesdays when the town fizzes with one of Mallorca's biggest fresh produce and livestock markets. Just off the town's main square, Sa Plaça.

Restaurant Ca'n Balaguer

c/Ciutat 19, Artà ☎971 835003. Good, old-fashioned restaurant specializing in traditional Catalan dishes – and an excellent place to try salted cod, long an island favourite. Reasonable prices too.

Restaurant El Puerto

Sa Llotja s/n, Colònia de Sant Jordi. Nothing too exciting, but this popular harbourfront spot divides into two: a café-bar offering bargain-basement pizza and spaghetti, and a restaurant specializing in seafood (at around €14 for a main course).

Restaurant Es Reco de Randa

c/Font 13, Randa ☎971 660997. Randa is a pretty little hamlet of old stone houses at the foot of Puig Randa, near Algaida, (see p.128). The village holds a three-star hotel, the *Es Reco de Randa*, and this has a delightful terraced restaurant, whose specialities include roast lamb and suckling pig. Main courses average around €20.

Restaurant Flamingo

c/Bordils s/n, Porto Cristo ☎971 822259. Closed Nov–Feb. Informal, popular restaurant with an outdoor terrace overlooking the ocean. The homemade paellas are delicious, or try the steamed mussels, or the mixed fish grill (€20).

Restaurant Florian

c/Cristóbal Colom 11, Porto Colom ☎971 824171. Immaculate restaurant offering a creative menu based on local ingredients and traditional dishes with a little extra vim and gusto. The outside terrace offers sea views and a good line in *tapas* is available at lunch times. Main courses average €20–25.

Restaurant La Fragua

c/Es Pla d'en Coset 3, Capdepera ☎971 565050. The classiest restaurant in Capdepera, this intimate, romantic spot serves delicious meals from a menu featuring mainland Spanish

dishes. It's located just off the main square, Plaça de L'Orient, on the way up towards the castle steps.

Restaurant Port Blau

c/Gabriel Roca 67, Colònia de Sant Jordi ☎971 656555. Closed Tues & Jan & Feb. Hogs the port's best location and lives up to its setting with some of the town's top food, including big, beautifully presented portions of the freshest fish, plus large salads and great bread. *Menú del día* is €10.25.

Restaurant Ses Rotges

c/Rafael Blanes 21, Cala Rajada ☎971 563108. Closed Nov–March. The pick of Cala Rajada's many restaurants in the hotel of the same name (see above). Fish is the speciality here with main courses hovering between €25–30.

▼RESTAURANT SES ROTGES

Shopping

Sineu market

Sineu. Wednesday all day. Sineu market is the largest livestock market on the island, and the one place where you're likely to spot the rare Mallorcan black pig – either in person or in a sausage. Cheese, fruit and veg stalls also, plus tourist knick-knacks. Get there early – say 8am – to avoid the crush.

Carnisseria Mary Carmen

c/Cristóbal Colom 35, Porto Colom ☎971 825005. Outstanding shop, that's a combination of butcher's, grocery and *traiteur*. One of their specialities is meat – top quality and locally produced. Also does a great line in pre-cooked, home-made meals. Closed Tues in winter.

Casa del Vino

Avgda Salvador Juan 73, Manacor ☎971 555165. Mon–Fri 10am–1.30pm & 5–7.30pm, Sat 10am–1pm. First-rate wine shop in the centre of Manacor specializing in Mallorcan vintages.

Ceramiques de Santanyí

c/Guardia Civil 22, Santanyí ☎971 163128. Mon–Fri 10am–1.30pm & 5–7.30pm, Sat 10am–1pm. Specialist producer of handmade ceramics, many with an especially pleasing metallic glaze.

Gordiola Glassworks

Ctra Palma–Manacor, km 19 ☎971 665046. June–Sept Mon–Sat 9am–8pm, Sun 9am–1.30pm; Oct–May Mon–Sat 9am–7pm, Sun 9am–1.30pm; free. Gordiola has been churning out glassware for a couple of hundred years (see p.148) and today's factory has a couple of large and well-stocked gift shops. Here, you'll find everything from the most abysmal tourist tat to works of great delicacy, notably green-tinted chandeliers of traditional Mallorcan design costing anything up to €3000.

Essentials

Arrival

The vast majority of visitors to Mallorca fly there, landing at the island's one and only international **airport**, a gleaming modern structure just 11km east of Palma, the capital. Palma is also the site of the island's main **ferry port** with services from the Spanish mainland and the other principal Balearic islands, Ibiza and Menorca. There are also ferries from Menorca to Port d'Alcúdia, on Mallorca's northern shore.

By plane

Mallorca's international airport has one enormous terminal, which handles both scheduled and charter flights, with separate floors for arrivals (downstairs) and departures (upstairs). Both floors have airport information desks – a good job, as the airport can be very confusing. On the arrivals floor, a flotilla of car rental outlets jostle for position by the luggage carousels. Beyond, through the glass doors, is the main arrivals hall, which has 24-hour ATMs and currency exchange facilities, plus a provincial tourist office (Mon–Sat 9am–10pm, Sun 9am–2pm) with oodles of information, including lists of hotels and *hostals*. They will not, however, help arrange (last-minute) accommodation and neither will most of the package-tour travel agents. An exception is the extremely helpful Prima Travel (☎971 680 505, ⊛www.prima-travel.com), who have a good selection of hotels, apartments and villas in all price ranges, plus English-speaking staff.

The least expensive way to get from the airport to Palma is by bus #1 (daily every 15min from 5.40am to 2.30am; €1.80), which leaves from the main entrance of the terminal building, just behind the taxi rank. These buses reach the city's inner ring road near the foot of Avinguda Gabriel Alomar i Villalonga, at the c/Joan Maragall junction, then head on to Plaça Espanya, on the north side of the centre, before continuing west to the Passeig Mallorca and then south to the top of Avinguda Jaume III. There are frequent stops along the way. A taxi from the airport to the city centre will set you back between €15–20.

By ferry

Two companies – Trasmediterranea and Balearia – run car ferry and seasonal catamaran services between mainland Spain and Mallorca with frequent daily sailings from Barcelona (ferry 8hr, catamaran 4hr 30min), Valencia (6–7 weekly; ferry 9hr, catamaran 6hr 15min) and Dénia (1 daily; ferry 10hr, catamaran 7hr). There are no services during part of the winter, usually from early December to the end of January. In addition, there's a Trasmediterranea car ferry from Maó, on Menorca, to Palma (1–2 weekly; 6hr) and Balearia runs two inter-island fast-ferry services to Port d'Alcúdia from Menorca, one from Maó, the other from Ciutadella. The route between Ibiza Town and Palma is served by both Trasmediterranea and Balearia (ferry: 2–3 daily; 4hr 30min; catamarans: 1–2 daily; 2hr 15min). Note that car rental firms on the Balearics do not allow their vehicles off their home island. Advance booking is strongly recommended on both car ferry and catamaran services. Tickets can be purchased at the port of embarkation or in advance by phone

---

Ferry companies

Balearia ☎902 160 180 (only Spanish spoken), ⊛www.balearia.net/eng.

Trasmediterranea ☎902 454 645, ⊛www.trasmediterranea.es (both English and Spanish spoken). The company's official UK agent is Southern Ferries, 179 Piccadilly, London W1V 9DB ☎020/7491 4968.

and via the companies' websites or with Trasmediterranea's UK agent (see box on p.151).

Palma ferry terminal is about 4km west of the city centre. Trasmediterranea ferries arrive at Terminal 2; Balearia ferries at Terminal 3, about 150m away. Bus #1 (5.40am–2.30am; €1.80) leaves every fifteen minutes from outside Terminal 2 to the Plaça Espanya. There are also taxi ranks outside both terminal buildings; the fare to the city centre is about €10. Port d'Alcúdia is about ten minutes' walk from the resort's main harbour-marina.

Information and websites

In Mallorca, the main provincial and municipal tourist offices are in Palma (see p.54). They will provide free maps of the town and the island, plus leaflets detailing all sorts of island-wide practicalities – from bus and train timetables to lists of car rental firms, ferry schedules and boat excursion organizers. Outside of Palma, many of the larger towns and resorts have seasonal tourist offices, but these vary enormously in quality, and while they are generally extremely useful for local information, they cannot be relied on to know anything about what goes on outside their patch. Opening hours vary considerably. The larger tourist offices are all open at least from Monday to Friday from 8 or 9am to 2 or 3pm. The smaller concerns operate from April or May to September or October, often on weekday mornings only.

As yet, the Internet hasn't really taken off in Mallorca. Many sites emanating from the islands are rudimentary and infrequently updated, and the majority are only available in Castilian (Spanish) or Catalan, though you can get help in deciphering these from any Internet translation service – for Spanish, try Ⓦ www.babelfish.altavista.com/translate .dyn. The main exception is the island's hotels, where having a website is becoming pretty much de rigeur.

Useful websites

Ⓦ **www.a-palma.es/eng** Useful site, providing detailed street maps, public transport information and "where to go" and "what's on" guides. Primarily in Spanish, but with English sections too, though some of the translations are incomplete.

Ⓦ **www.baleares.com** A multilingual tourist guide to all the Balearics with separate sections devoted to a whole raft of special features from art through to cycling and car rental. The site's poorly laid out, but the information it contains is good – once you find it.

Ⓦ **www.conselldemallorca.net** One of the best-presented Mallorcan sites, though in Catalan only. Contains all sorts of information and news, and has a useful events page, *Novetats*, although the translation produced by Babelfish (see above) is rather garbled.

Ⓦ **www.inm.es/wwb** Daily weather forecasts for the whole of Spain – in Spanish.

Ⓦ **www.malhigh.com** Expat heaven, this site hosts private ads from German and English expatriates. Useful and amusing in equal measure.

Maps

Detailed road maps of Mallorca are widely available from island newsagents, petrol stations, souvenir shops and bookshops. There are several different types on offer and prices vary considerably, but you shouldn't have to pay more than €5. If you do buy a map, it's important to get a Catalan version: all island road, town and street signs are in Catalan, but many of the maps on sale are in Castilian (Spanish) and are, therefore, impossibly confusing to use. To ensure you're buying a Catalan map, check out the spelling of Port de Pollença on Mallorca's north coast; if it reads "Puerto de Pollença", you've got a Castilian version. The most accurate Catalan road map is Michelin's *Balears* (Number 579 Regional; 1:140,000). A useful supplement is the *Mallorca* map (1:150,000) produced by the Ministerio de Obras Públicas (Ministry of Public Works). The Michelin map is widely available; the Public Works map can be bought at the one specialist map shop in Palma (see p.72). Note, however, that both have inaccuracies and neither provides a detailed map of Palma. The best maps of Palma are available for free from the city's tourist offices.

Serious hikers are poorly provided for. There are no really reliable maps of the island's hiking trails, though the cartographic void has been partly filled by Discovery Walking Guides (ⓦ www .walking.demon.co.uk), whose publications include the very competent *Mallorca North & Mountains Tour & Trail Map* (1:40,000) and the *Mallorca North Walking Guide* (1:40,000). These are not widely available on Mallorca, so pick up a copy before you set out, either from your local bookshop or Amazon (ⓦ www .amazon.co.uk).

Transport

Mallorca has a reliable bus network between all its major settlements, a multitude of taxis, a plethora of car rental firms, plenty of bicycles and mopeds to rent, as well as a couple of very useful train lines.

Buses

Palma is the hub of the island's extensive network and from here it's possible to reach most of the villages and resorts of the coast and interior with ease. These main routes are supplemented by more intermittent local services between the smaller towns of the interior and between neighbouring resorts.

Buses in Palma and the adjacent Bay of Palma resorts are all operated by EMT (Empresa Municipal de Transports; see box below); the rest of the island is served by a bewildering range of bus companies, though their services are co-ordinated by tib (Transports de les Illes Balears; see box below). There is an excellent tib bus information centre at the main bus station in Palma, a few minutes' walk from the Plaça Espanya.

As for ticket prices, distances are small – it is, for example, only 110km from Andratx in the west to Cala Rajada in the east – and consequently travel costs are low: the one-way fare from Palma to Colònia de Sant Jordi, for instance, is just €5.50.

Passengers buy tickets from the driver, unless they've been bought in advance at a bus station. For the most part, bus stops are clearly indicated with brightly coloured signs, but in some of the country towns and villages they can be very

Bus and train information

For bus timetable information in Palma and the Bay of Palma, call EMT ☎971 214444 (press 1 after the pre-recorded message in Catalan, and you'll get an operator who might speak a bit of English), or check ⊛www.a-palma.es. Outside of Palma and its environs, call tib ☎971 177777 (Spanish and Catalan only).

The Palma–Sóller train has its own information line and website, ☎902 364711, ⊛www.trendesoller.com. For timetable information on the Palma–Inca–sa Pobla/Manacor line, call ☎971 177777 (again, Spanish and Catalan only).

hard to find. Remember also that bus services are drastically reduced on Sundays and holidays, and it's best not even to consider travelling out into the sticks on these days. The Catalan words to look out for on timetables are *diari* (daily), *feiners* (workdays, including Saturday), *diumenge* (Sunday) and *festius* (holidays). Local bus timetables are available at most tourist offices.

Trains

Mallorca has its own, narrow-gauge train network. One line travels through the mountains from Palma to Sóller (28km). The second shuttles across the flatlands of the interior from Palma to Binissalem and then Inca, just beyond which it forks, with one branch nudging south to Sineu, Petra and Manacor, the other pushing on to Sa Pobla. Work is underway to extend the line from Sa Pobla to Alcúdia. Each line has its own station in Palma and these sit alongside each other on Plaça Espanya. The trip to Sóller (see p.86) takes about an hour and a quarter and passes through some of the islands' most magnificent scenery. The Inca line is much less enjoyable, but the service is much more frequent with three or four departures hourly. It takes forty minutes to get from Palma to Inca, twenty minutes more to Sa Pobla. The standard return fare from Palma to Sa Pobla is around €6.

Car rental

Car rental companies (*coches de alquiler*) throng the island's resorts, larger towns and airport. All the major international players have outlets, and there are dozens of small, local companies too.

To rent a car, you'll have to be 21 or over (and have been driving for at least a year), and you'll probably need a credit card – though some places will accept a hefty deposit in cash and some smaller companies simply ignore all the normal regulations. If you're planning to spend much time driving on rougher tracks, you'll probably be better off with a moped, or even a four-wheel-drive vehicle (about thirty percent more expensive than the average car and available from larger rental agencies).

Cycling

Cycling can be an inexpensive and flexible way of getting around Mallorca, though you have to be pretty fit to tackle the steep hills of the northern part of the island. The Spanish are keen cycling fans, which means that you'll (usually) find reasonable facilities and respectful car drivers.

The main tourist office in Palma (see p.54) produces a free specialist leaflet, the *Guía del Ciclista* (in Spanish only), which details suggested itineraries and indicates distances and levels of difficulty. The website ⊛ www.baleares .com/tourist.guide/cycling gives details in several languages, including English, of eight different cycle routes on Mallorca, from 70km to 320km. Routes are designed to avoid busy roads and to provide sections on the flat as well as steep climbs.

Renting a bike costs anywhere between about €5 and €8 a day for an ordinary bike (€27 to €40 per week), or about thirty percent more for a mountain bike. Renting is straightforward: there are dozens of suppliers (there's usually one at every resort) and tourist offices can provide a list or advise you of the nearest outlet.

Moped rental

Mopeds (scooters) are a popular means of transport, especially for visiting remoter spots, and are widely available. Prices start at about €15 per day, including insurance and crash helmets, which must be worn. Be warned, however, that the insurance often excludes theft – always check with the company first. You will generally be asked to show some kind of driving licence (particularly for mopeds over 50cc) and to leave a deposit on your credit card, though most places will accept cash as an alternative.

Accommodation

Package-tour operators have a stranglehold on thousands of Mallorcan hotel rooms, villas and apartments, but nevertheless reasonably priced rooms are still available to the independent traveller, though options can be limited at the height of the season, when advance reservations are strongly recommended. Most hoteliers speak at least a modicum of English, so visitors who don't speak Catalan or Spanish can usually book over the phone, but a confirmation letter or email is always a good idea. In Mallorca the easiest place to get a room is Palma, with Sóller and Port de Sóller lagging not far behind, and there are usually vacancies at the five island monasteries that offer frugal accommodation in remote hilltop locations.

Types of accommodation

It's often worth bargaining over hotel room prices, especially outside peak season, since the posted tariff doesn't necessarily mean much. Many hotels have rooms at different prices, and tend to offer the more expensive ones first. Most places also have rooms with three or four beds at not a great deal more than the price of a double room, which represents a real saving for families and small groups. On the other hand, people travelling alone invariably end up paying over the odds.

Incidentally, many establishments are signed as *hostals*, though there is little difference between a *hostal* and a (less expensive) hotel.

Fincas

Many of Mallorca's old stone *fincas* (farmhouses) have been snaffled up for use as second homes, and some are now leased by their owners to package-tour operators for the whole or part of the season – Individual Traveller's Spain (UK ☎08700/780194, ✆ www.indiv-travellers.com) has one of the best selections. Out of the tour operators' main season, these *fincas* often stand idle.

At any time of the year, though preferably well in advance of your holiday, it's worth approaching the Associació Agroturisme Balear, Avgda Gabriel Alomar i Villalonga 8a–2a, 07006 Palma (☎971 721508, ✆ www.agroturismo-balear.com), which issues a booklet detailing most of the finest *fincas* and takes bookings. Although some *fincas* are modest affairs and still a part of working farms, the majority are comparatively luxurious and many are situated in remote and beautiful spots. They are not, however, cheap: prices range from €40 to €80 per person per night, and a minimum length of stay of anything between two nights and two weeks is often stipulated.

Sports and activities

During the day at least, tourist life on Mallorca is centred on the beach. There are long and generous strands at several of the major resorts – such as Port d'Alcúdia, S'Arenal and Port de Pollença – and several dozen much smaller cove **beaches**, like the ones at Deià and Estellencs. At all the larger resorts, an army of companies offer equipment hire for a wide range of beach sports and activities, from **sailing** and pedaloe pedalling through to jet skiing and **windsurfing**. There are sandcastle-building competitions too, as well as some scuba diving, though the underwater world off Mallorca lacks colour and clarity – the best **diving** is around the islet of Sa Dragonera and off Cala Figuera on the east coast. If you're keen to participate in any of these activities, there's no need to make advance reservations – just turn up early(ish) in the morning and off you go.

Away from the coast, **cycling** is a popular pastime (see p.154) as is **horse and pony riding** – indeed, Mallorca is dotted with stables and crisscrossed by bridle paths. Even more popular, however, is **hiking**, with hundreds of hikers descending on the Serra de Tramuntana mountains in the spring and autumn, necessarily out of the heat of the summer sun. It is also encouraging to note that the island's hiking trails, which were once notorious for their poor signage, are in the process of being re-signed.

Useful contacts for sport and activities

Hiking: Headwater (UK ☎01606/720099, ⊛www.headwater.com) is a well-regarded walking-tour specialist providing guided hikes in the Serra de Tramuntana mountains. Their standard eight-day guided hike takes place from mid-September to November and from February to April.

Horse riding: A full list of Mallorcan horse-riding companies is provided on ⊛www.mallorcaonline.com/sport/equitau.htm.

Sailing & Windsurfing: Sail & Surf Pollença (☎971 865346, ⊛www.sailsurf.de). Well-regarded, German-run specialists in sailing and windsurfing.

Festivals

January
16: Revetla de Sant Antoni Abat (Eve of St Antony's Day) is celebrated by the lighting of bonfires (*foguerons*) in Palma and several of Mallorca's villages, especially Sa Pobla and Muro. In the latter, the villagers move from fire to fire, dancing round in fancy dress and eating *espinagades*, traditional eel and vegetable patties.

17: Beneides de Sant Antoni (Blessing of St Antony). St Antony's feast day is marked by processions in many of Mallorca's country towns, notably Sa Pobla and Artà, with farmyard animals herded through the streets to receive the saint's blessing and protection against disease.

19: Revetla de Sant Sebastià Palma has more bonfires, singing and dancing for St Sebastian.

20: Festa de Sant Sebastià Pollença procession led by a holy banner (*estenard*) picturing the saint. It's accompanied by *cavallets* (literally "merry-go-rounds"), two young dancers each wearing a cardboard horse and imitating the animal's walk. You'll see *cavallets*, which are of medieval origin, at many of the island's festivals.

February

Carnaval Lots of towns and villages live it up during the week before Lent with marches and fancy dress parades. The biggest and liveliest is in Palma, where the shindig is known as *Sa Rua* (the Cavalcade).

March/April

Setmana Santa (Holy Week) is as widely observed in Mallorca as it is everywhere else in Spain. On **Maundy Thursday** in Palma, a much venerated icon of the crucified Christ, *La Sang*, is taken from the eponymous church on the Plaça del Hospital (off La Rambla) and paraded through the city streets. There are also solemn **Good Friday** (*Divendres Sant*) processions in many towns and villages, with the more important taking place in Palma and Sineu. Most holy of all, however, is the Good Friday *Davallament* (The Lowering), the culmination of Holy Week in Pollença. Here, in total silence and by torchlight, the inhabitants lower a figure of Christ down from the hilltop Oratori to the church of Nostra Senyora dels Àngels. During Holy Week there are also many *romerias* (pilgrimages) to the island's holy places, with one of the most popular being the climb up to the Ermita Santa Magdalena, near Inca. The Monestir de Lluc, which possesses Mallorca's most venerated shrine, is another religious focus during this time, with the penitential trudging round its Camí dels Misteris del Rosari (The Way of the Mysteries of the Rosary).

May

Mid-May: Sa Firá i Es Firó in Port de Sóller features mock battles between Christians and infidels in commemoration of the thrashing of a band of Arab pirates in 1561. Lots of booze and firing of antique rifles into the air.

June

Early to mid-June: Corpus Christi At noon in the main square of Pollença an ancient and curious dance of uncertain provenance takes place – the *Ball de les Àguiles* (Dance of the Eagles) – followed by a religious procession.

July

Last Sunday: Festa de Sant Jaume This festival in Alcúdia celebrates the feast day of St James with a popular religious procession followed by folk dances, fireworks and the like.

August

2: Mare de Déu dels Àngels Moors and Christians battle it out again, this time in Pollença.
20: Cavallet (see above). Dances in Felanitx.

September

Second week: Nativitat de Nostra Senyora (Nativity of the Virgin). In Alaró, honouring the Virgin with a pilgrimage to a hilltop shrine near the Castell d'Alaró.

December

Christmas (*Nadal*) is especially picturesque in Palma and Ciutadella, where there are Nativity plays in the days leading up to the 25th.

Public holidays

January 1 New Year's Day (Cap d'Any in Catalan, Año Nuevo in Castilian)
January 6 Epiphany (Epifania del Senyor)
March 19 St Joseph's Day (Sant Josep)
Good Friday Divendres Sant (Viernes Santo in Castilian)
May 1 Labour Day (Festa del Treball)
Early or mid-June Corpus Christi
June 24 St John's Day (Sant Joan), King Juan Carlos's name-day
June 29 St Peter and St Paul Day (Sant Pere i Sant Pau)

July 25 St James's Day (Santiago)
August 15 Assumption of the Virgin (L'Assumpció)
October 12 Discovery of America Day (Día de la Hispanidad)
November 1 All Saints (Tots Sants)
December 6 Constitution Day (Día de la Constitució)
December 8 Immaculate Conception (Inmaculada Concepció)
December 25 Christmas Day (Nadal in Catalan; Navidad in Castilian)

Directory

Addresses These are usually abbreviated to a standard format – "c/Bellver 7" translates as Bellver Street (carrer) no. 7. Plaça means square. "Plaça Rosari 5, 2è" means the left-hand door from the staircase on the second floor at no. 5. "Passeig d'es Born 15, 1–C" means suite C, first floor, at no. 15. "s/n" (sense número) indicates a building without a street number. In Franco's day, most avenues and boulevards were named after Fascist heroes and, although the vast majority were rechristened years ago, there's still some confusion in remoter spots. Another source of bafflement can be house numbers: some houses carry more than one number (the by-product of half-hearted reorganizations), and on many streets the sequence is impossible to fathom.

Children Most hotels, pensions and *hostals* welcome children and many offer rooms with three or four beds. Restaurants and cafés almost always encourage families too. Many package holidays have child-minding facilities as part of the deal. Disposable nappies and other basic supplies are widely available in the resort areas and the larger towns.

Disabilities, Travellers with Despite its popularity as a holiday destination, Mallorca pays scant regard to its disabled visitors, with facilities lagging way behind those of many EU countries. That said, things are slowly improving. Hotels with wheelchair access and other appropriate facilities are increasingly common and, by law, all new public buildings in Spain are required to be fully accessible. Transport is particularly problematic, as buses are not equipped for wheelchairs, and few of the islands' car rental firms have vehicles with adaptations – though at least the taxi drivers are usually helpful.

Doctors and dentists In the resort areas and in Palma most hotel receptions will be able to find an English-speaking doctor or dentist. For complete lists look under *metges* (Castilian *médicos*) or *clíniques dentals* (*clínicas dentales*) in the *Yellow Pages*.

Electricity The current is 220 volts AC, with standard European-style two-pin plugs. Brits will need an adaptor to connect their appliances, North Americans both an adaptor and a 220-to-110 transformer.

Emergencies For medical, fire and police emergencies, call ☏112.

Internet Many of Mallorca's better hotels provide free Internet access for their guests. Internet cafés are thin on the ground, but Palma has a couple including *Cyber Central*, in the city centre at c/Soledad 4.

Mail The Mallorcan postal system is competent and comprehensive, with post offices (*correus*) located in every town and most larger villages. Opening hours are usually Monday to Friday 9am to 2pm, though the main post office in Palma is open through the afternoon and on Saturday mornings too. All post offices close on public holidays.

Mobile phones Mobile phone access is routine in all the larger towns and villages and in most of the countryside. Mallorca's mobile network works on GSM 900/1800, which means that mobiles bought in North America need to be triband to gain cellular access.

Money Spanish currency is the euro (€). Each euro is made up of 100 cents. Notes come in denominations of 5, 10, 50 and 500 euros, coins as 1, 2, 5, 10, 20 and 50 cents, and 1 and 2 euros. The exchange rate for the euro at time of writing was 0.70 to the British pound, 1.15 to the US dollar, 1.51 to the Canadian dollar, 1.61 to the Australian dollar and 1.84 to the NZ dollar. ATMs are commonplace, especially in the cities and larger resorts, and are undoubtedly the quickest and easiest way of getting money. Most ATMs give instructions in a variety of languages, and accept a host of debit cards, including all those carrying the Cirrus coding. Credit cards can be used in ATMs too, but in this case transactions are treated as loans, with interest accruing daily from the date of withdrawal. All major credit cards, including American Express, Visa and MasterCard, are widely accepted in Mallorca.

Opening hours Although there's been some movement towards a northern European working day – especially in

Palma and the major tourist resorts – most shops and offices still close for a siesta of at least two hours in the hottest part of the afternoon between 1/2pm and 4/5pm. Cafés and *tapas* bars open from around 9am until at least early in the evening, and many remain open till late at night. Restaurants open from around noon until sometime between 2pm and 4pm, before reopening in the evening from around 7/8pm until 10/11pm. Those restaurants with their eye on the tourist trade often stay open all day and can be relied upon on Sundays, when many local spots close.

Telephones You can make domestic and international telephone calls with equal ease from Spanish public (and private) phones. Most hotel rooms also have phones, but note that there is almost always an exorbitant surcharge for their use. For international operator assistance within the EU call ☏1008, ☏1005 for rest of the world. Directory enquiries are on ☏11811. To call Mallorca from abroad, dial your international access code, fol-lowed by ☏34 for Spain and then the nine-digit local number. Note that all Bal-earic phone numbers begin with ☏971, but this is an integral part of the number, not an area code.

Time Spain (and therefore Mallorca) is one hour ahead of Greenwich Mean Time, six hours ahead of US Eastern Standard Time, nine hours ahead of US Pacific Standard Time, nine hours behind Aus-tralian Eastern Standard Time and eleven hours behind New Zealand – except for periods during the changeovers made in the respective countries to and from daylight saving. In Spain, the clocks go forward an hour on the last Sunday of March and back an hour on the last Sun-day of October.

Visas and red tape Citizens of the UK, Ireland and other EU countries – as well as nationals of Australia, New Zealand, Canada and the US – only need a valid passport to enter Spain for up to ninety days. Your passport must be valid for the entire period of the visit.

Language

Language

Although Catalan is the preferred language of most islanders, you'll almost always get by perfectly well if you speak Castilian (Spanish), as long as you're aware of the use of Catalan in timetables and so forth. Once you get into it, Castilian is one of the easiest languages there is, the rules of pronunciation pretty straightforward and strictly observed. You'll find some basic pronunciation rules below for both Catalan and Castilian, and a selection of words and phrases in both languages. Castilian is certainly easier to pronounce, but don't be afraid to try Catalan, especially in the more out-of-the-way places – you'll generally get a good reception if you at least try communicating in the local language.

On paper, Catalan looks like a cross between French and Spanish and is generally easy to understand if you know those two, although when spoken it has a very harsh sound and is far harder to come to grips with.

Numerous Spanish phrasebooks and dictionaries are available. The most user-friendly is Rough Guide's *Spanish Dictionary Phrasebook*. No English–Catalan phrasebook is currently in print and there's only one dictionary, published by Routledge

Castilian (Spanish): a few rules

Unless there's an accent, words ending in d, l, r, and z are **stressed** on the last syllable, all others on the second to last. All **vowels** are pure and short; combinations have predictable results.

A   somewhere between back and father.

E   as in get.

I   as in police.

O   as in hot.

U   as in rule.

C   is lisped before E and I, hard otherwise: *cerca* is pronounced "thairka".

CH   is pronounced as in English.

G   is a guttural H sound (like the *ch* in loch) before E or I, a hard G elsewhere: *gigante* is pronounced "higante".

H   is always silent.

J   is the same sound as a guttural G: *jamón* is pronounced "hamon".

LL   sounds like an English Y: *tortilla* is pronounced "torteeya".

N	as in English, unless it has a tilde (ñ) over it, when it becomes NY: *mañana* sounds like "man-yaana".
QU	is pronounced like an English K.
R	is rolled, RR doubly so.
V	sounds more like B, *vino* becoming "beano".
X	has an S sound before consonants, a KS sound before vowels.
Z	is the same as a soft C, so *cerveza* is pronounced "thairvaitha".

Catalan: a few rules

With *Català*, don't be tempted to use the few rules of Castilian pronunciation you may know – in particular the soft Spanish Z and C don't apply, so unlike in the rest of Spain it's not "Barthelona" but "Barcelona", as in English.

A	as in hat if stressed, as in alone when unstressed.
E	varies, but usually as in get.
I	as in police.
IG	sounds like the "tch" in the English scratch; *lleig* (ugly) is pronounced "yeah-tch".
O	varies, but usually as in hot.
U	lies somewhere between put and rule.
Ç	sounds like an English S: *plaça* is pronounced "plassa".
C	followed by an E or I is soft; otherwise hard.
G	followed by E or I is like the "zh" in Zhivago; otherwise hard.
H	is always silent.
J	as in the French "Jean".
LL	sounds like an English Y or LY, like the "yuh" sound in "million".
N	as in English, though before F or V it sometimes sounds like an M.
NY	replaces the Castilian Ñ.
QU	before E or I sounds like K; before A or O as in "quit".
R	is rolled, but only at the start of a word; at the end it's often silent.
T	is pronounced as in English, though sometimes it sounds like a D, as in *viatge* or *dotze*.
TX	is like the English CH.
V	at the start of a word sounds like B; in all other positions it's a soft F sound.
W	is pronounced like a B/V.
X	is like SH in most words, though in some, like exit, it sounds like an X.
Z	is like the English Z.

Useful words and phrases

Basics

ENGLISH	SPANISH	CATALAN
Yes, No, OK	**Sí, No, Vale**	Si, No, Val
Please, Thank you	**Por favor, Gracias**	Per favor, Gràcies
Where, When	**Dónde, Cuándo**	On, Quan
What, How much	**Qué, Cuánto**	Què, Quant
Here, There	**Aquí, Allí, Allá**	Aquí, Allí, Allà
This, That	**Esto, Eso**	Això, Allò
Now, Later	**Ahora, Más tarde**	Ara, Més tard
Open, Closed	**Abierto/a, Cerrado/a**	Obert, Tancat
With, Without	**Con, Sin**	Amb, Sense
Good, Bad	**Buen(o)/a, Mal(o)/a**	Bo(na), Dolent(a)
Big, Small	**Gran(de), Pequeño/a**	Gran, Petit(a)
Cheap, Expensive	**Barato/a, Caro/a**	Barat(a), Car(a)
Hot, Cold	**Caliente, Frío/a**	Calent(a), Fred(a)
More, Less	**Más, Menos**	Més, Menys
Today, Tomorrow	**Hoy, Mañana**	Avui, Demà
Yesterday	**Ayer**	Ahir
Day before yesterday	**Anteayer**	Abans-d'ahir
Next week	**La semana que viene**	La setmana que ve
Next month	**El mes que viene**	El mes que ve

Greetings and responses

ENGLISH	SPANISH	CATALAN
Hello, Goodbye	**Hola, Adiós**	Hola, Adéu
Good morning	**Buenos días**	Bon dia
Good afternoon/night	**Buenas tardes/noches**	Bona tarda/nit
See you later	**Hasta luego**	Fins després
Sorry	**Lo siento/discúlpeme**	Ho sento
Excuse me	**Con permiso/perdón**	Perdoni
How are you?	**¿Cómo está (usted)?**	*Com va?*
I (don't) understand	**(No) Entiendo**	(No) Ho entenc
Not at all/You're welcome	**De nada**	De res
Do you speak English?	**¿Habla (usted) inglés?**	Parla anglès?
I (don't) speak	**(No) Hablo Español**	(No) Parlo Català
My name is . . .	**Me llamo . . .**	Em dic . . .
What's your name?	**¿Cómo se llama usted?**	Com es diu?
I am English	**Soy inglés/esa**	Sóc anglès/esa
Scottish	**escocés/esa**	escocès/esa
Australian	**australiano/a**	australià/ana
Canadian	**canadiense/a**	canadenc(a)
American	**americano/a**	americà/ana
Irish	**irlandés/esa**	irlandès/esa
Welsh	**galés/esa**	gallès/esa

Hotels and transport

ENGLISH	SPANISH	CATALAN
I want	**Quiero**	Vull (pronounced "fwee")
I'd like	**Quisiera**	Voldria

English	Spanish	Catalan
Do you know . . . ?	¿Sabe . . . ?	Vostès saben . . . ?
I don't know	No sé	No sé
There is (is there?)	(¿)Hay(?)	Hi ha(?)
Give me . . .	Deme . . .	Doneu-me . . .
Do you have . . . ?	¿Tiene . . . ?	Té . . . ?
. . . the time	. . . la hora	. . . l'hora
. . . a room	. . . una habitación	. . . alguna habitació
. . . with two beds/ double bed	. . . con dos camas/ cama matrimonial	. . . amb dos llits/ llit per dues persones
. . . with shower/bath	. . . con ducha/baño	. . . amb dutxa/bany
for one person (two people)	para una persona (dos personas)	per a una persona (dues persones)
for one night (one week)	para una noche (una semana)	per una nit (una setmana)
It's fine, how much is it?	Está bien, ¿cuánto es?	Esta bé, quant és?
It's too expensive	Es demasiado caro	És massa car
Don't you have anything cheaper?	¿No tiene algo más barato?	En té de més bon preu?
Can one . . . ?	¿Se puede . . . ?	Es pot . . . ?
. . . camp (near) here?	¿ . . . acampar aquí (cerca)?	. . . acampar a la vora?
Is there a hostel nearby?	¿Hay un hostal aquí cerca?	Hi ha un hostal a la vora?
It's not very far	No es muy lejos	No és gaire lluny
How do I get to . . . ?	¿Por dónde se va a . . . ?	Per anar a . . . ?
Left, right, straight on	Izquierda, derecha, todo recto	A l'esquerra, a la dreta, tot recte
Where is . . . ?	¿Dónde está . . . ?	On és . . . ?
. . . the bus station	. . . la estación de autobuses	. . . l'estació de autobuses
. . . the bus stop	. . . la parada	. . . la parada
. . . the railway station	. . . la estación de ferrocarril	. . . l'estació
. . . the nearest bank	. . . el banco más cercano	. . . el banc més a prop
. . . the post office	. . . el correo/ la oficina de correos	. . . l'oficina de correus
. . . the toilet	. . . el baño/aseo/servicio	. . . la toaleta
Where does the bus to . . . leave from?	¿De dónde sale el autobús para . . . ?	De on surt el autobús a . . . ?
Is this the train for Barcelona?	¿Es este el tren para Barcelona?	Aquest tren va a Barcelona?
I'd like a (return) ticket to . . .	Quisiera un billete (de ida y vuelta) para . .	Voldria un bitllet (d'anar i tornar) a . . .
What time does it leave (arrive in . . .)?	¿A qué hora sale (llega a . . .)?	A quina hora surt (arriba a . . .)?
What is there to eat?	¿Qué hay para comer?	Què hi ha per menjar?
What's that?	¿Qué es eso?	Què és això?

Days of the week

ENGLISH	SPANISH	CATALAN
Monday	lunes	dilluns
Tuesday	martes	dimarts
Wednesday	miércoles	dimecres
Thursday	jueves	dijous
Friday	viernes	divendres
Saturday	sábado	dissabte
Sunday	domingo	diumenge

Numbers

	SPANISH	CATALAN
1	un/uno/una	un(a)
2	dos	dos (dues)
3	tres	tres
4	cuatro	quatre
5	cinco	cinc
6	seis	sis
7	siete	set
8	ocho	vuit
9	nueve	nou
10	diez	deu
11	once	onze
12	doce	dotze
13	trece	tretze
14	catorce	catorze
15	quince	quinze
16	dieciséis	setze
17	diecisiete	disset
18	dieciocho	divuit
19	diecinueve	dinou
20	veinte	vint
21	veintiuno	vint-i-un
30	treinta	trenta
40	cuarenta	quaranta
50	cincuenta	cinquanta
60	sesenta	seixanta
70	setenta	setanta
80	ochenta	vuitanta
90	noventa	novanta
100	cien(to)	cent
101	ciento uno	cent un
102	ciento dos	cent dos (dues)
200	doscientos	dos-cents (dues-centes)
500	quinientos	cinc-cents
1000	mil	mil
2000	dos mil	dos mil

Food and drink

In this section, we've generally given the **Catalan** names for food and drink items, since (dialects of) Catalan are the islanders' first language. Most restaurants, cafés and bars have **multilingual menus**, including English, but out in the countryside in cheaper cafés and restaurants there may only be a Catalan menu or maybe no menu at all, in which case the waiter will rattle off the day's dishes in Catalan. You'll occasionally find menus in **Castilian** (Spanish), which is understood by almost all restaurant staff, and we've given Castilian names alongside Catalan ones wherever useful.

Basics

ENGLISH	CATALAN	CASTILIAN
Bread	Pa	Pan
Butter	Mantega	Mantequilla
Cheese	Formatge	Queso
Eggs	Ous	Huevos
Oil	Oli	Aceite
Pepper	Pebre	Pimienta
Salt	Sal	Sal
Sugar	Sucre	Azúcar
Vinegar	Vinagre	Vinagre
Garlic	All	Ajo
Rice	Arròs	Arroz
Fruit	Fruita	Fruta
Vegetables	Verdures/Llegumos	Verduras/Legumbres
To have breakfast	Esmorzar	Desayunar
To have lunch	Dinar	Almorzar
Sopar	Cenar	To have dinner
Menu	Menú	Carta
Bottle	Ampolla	Botella
Glass	Got	Vaso
Fork	Forquilla	Tenedor
Knife	Ganivet	Cuchillo
Spoon	Cullera	Cuchara
Table	Taula	Mesa
The bill/check	El compte	La cuenta
Grilled	A la planxa	A la brasa
Fried	Fregit	Frit
Stuffed/rolled	Farcit	Relleno
Casserole	Guisat	Guisado
Roast	Rostit	Asado

Fruit (fruita) and vegetables (verdures/llegumes)

ENGLISH	CATALAN	CASTILIAN
Apple	Poma	Manzana
Asparagus	Espàrrecs	Espárragos
Aubergine/eggplant	Albergínies	Berenjenas
Banana	Plàtan	Plátano
Carrots	Pastanagues	Zanahorias
Cucumber	Concombre	Pepino
Grapes	Raïm	Uvas
Melon	Meló	Melón
Mushrooms	Xampinyons (also bolets, setes)	Champiñones
Onions	Cebes	Cebollas
Orange	Taronja	Naranja
Potatoes	Patates	Patatas
Pear	Pera	Pera
Peas	Pèsols	Arvejas
Pineapple	Pinya	Piña
Peach	Préssec	Melocotón
Strawberries	Maduixes	Fresas
Tomatoes	Tomàquets	Tomates

Bocadillos fillings

ENGLISH	CATALAN	CASTILIAN
Catalan sausage	Butifarra	Butifarra
Cheese	Formatge	Queso
Cooked ham	Cuixot dolç	Jamón York
Cured ham	Pernil salat	Jamón serrano
Loin of pork	Llom	Lomo
Omelette	Truita	Tortilla
Salami	Salami	Salami
Sausage	Salxitxó	Salchichón
Spicy sausage	Xoriç	Chorizo
Tuna	Tonyina	Atún

Tapas and racions

CATALAN	CASTILIAN	ENGLISH
Anxoves	Boquerones	Anchovies
Bollit	Cocido	Stew
Calamars	Calamares	Squid, usually deep-fried in rings
Calamars amb tinta	Calamares en su tinta	Squid in ink
Cargols	Caracoles	Snails, often served in a spicy/curry sauce
Cargols de mar	Berberechos	Cockles (shellfish)
Calamarins	Chipirones	Whole baby squid
Carn amb salsa	Carne en salsa	Meat in tomato sauce
Croqueta	Croqueta	Fish or chicken croquette
Empanada petita	Empanadilla	Fish or meat pasty
Ensalada russa	Ensaladilla	Russian salad (diced vegetables in mayonnaise)
Escalibada	Escalibada	Aubergine (eggplant) and pepper salad
Faves	Habas	Broad beans
Faves amb cuixot	Habas con jamón	Beans with ham
Fetge	Hígado	Liver
Gambes	Gambas	Prawns
Musclos	Mejillones	Mussels (either steamed, or served with diced tomatoes and onion)
Navallas	Navajas	Razor clams
Olives	Aceitunas	Olives
Ou bollit	Huevo cocido	Hard-boiled egg
Pa amb tomàquet	Pan con tomate	Bread, rubbed with tomato and oil
Patates amb all i oli	Patatas alioli	Potatoes in garlic mayonnaise
Patates cohentes	Patatas bravas	Fried potato cubes with spicy sauce and mayonnaise
Pilotes	Albóndigas	Meatballs, usually in sauce

Pinxo	**Pincho moruno**	Kebab
Pop	**Pulpo**	Octopus
Prebes	**Pimientos**	Sweet (bell) peppers
Ronyons amb xeres	**Riñones al jerez**	Kidneys in sherry
Sardines	**Sardinas**	Sardines
Sípia	**Sepia**	Cuttlefish
Tripa	**Callos**	Tripe
Truita espanyola	**Tortilla española**	Potato omelette
Truita francesa	**Tortilla francesa**	Plain omelette
Tumbet	**Tumbet**	Pepper, potato, pumpkin and aubergine (eggplant) stew with tomato purée
Xampinyons	**Champiñones**	Mushrooms, usually fried in garlic
Xoriç	**Chorizo**	Spicy sausage

Balearic dishes and specialities

Many of the specialities that follow come from the Balearics' shared history with Catalunya. The more elaborate fish and meat dishes are usually limited to the fancier restaurants.

SAUCES

Salsa mahonesa	Mayonnaise
Allioli	Garlic mayonnaise
Salsa romesco	Spicy tomato and wine sauce to accompany fish (from Tarragona)

SOUPS (SOPA), STARTERS AND SALADS (AMANIDA)

Amanida catalana	Salad with sliced meat and cheese
Carn d'olla	Mixed meat soup
Entremesos	Starter of mixed meat and cheese
Escalivada	Aubergine/eggplant, pepper and onion salad
Escudella	Mixed vegetable soup
Espinacs a la Catalana	Spinach with raisins and pine nuts
Esqueixada	Dried cod salad with peppers, tomatoes, onions and olives
Fideus a la cassola	Baked vermicelli with meat
Llenties guisades	Stewed lentils
Pa amb oli	Bread rubbed with olive oil, eaten with ham, cheese or fruit
Samfaina	Ratatouille-like stew of onions, peppers, aubergine/ eggplant and tomato
Sopa d'all	Garlic soup
Sopas mallorquínas	Vegetable soup, sometimes with meat and chickpeas (garbanzos)
Truita (d'alls tendres; de xampinyons; de patates)	Omelette/tortilla (with garlic; with mushrooms; with potato). Be sure you're ordering omelette (tortilla), not trout (truita).

RICE DISHES

Arròs negre	"Black rice", cooked with squid ink
Arròs a banda	Rice with seafood, the rice served separately
Arròs a la marinera	Paella: rice with seafood and saffron
Paella a la Catalana	Mixed meat and seafood paella, sometimes distinguished from a seafood paella by being called Paella a Valencia

MEAT (CARN)

Albergínies en es forn	Aubergines/eggplants stuffed with grilled meat
Botifarra amb mongetes	Spicy blood sausage with white beans
Conill (all i oli)	Rabbit (with garlic mayonnaise)
Escaldum	Chicken and potato stew in an almond sauce
Estofat de vedella	Veal stew
Fetge	Liver
Fricandó	Veal casserole
Frito mallorquín	Pigs' offal, potatoes and onions cooked with oil
Mandonguilles	Meatballs, usually in a sauce with peas
Perdius a la vinagreta	Partridge in vinegar gravy
Pollastre (farcit; amb gambas; al cava)	Chicken (stuffed; with prawns; cooked in sparkling wine)
Porc (rostit)	Pork (roast)
Sobrasada	Finely minced pork sausage, flavoured with paprika

FISH (PEIX) AND SHELLFISH (MARISC)

Bacallà (amb samfaina)	Dried cod (with ratatouille)
Caldereta de llagosta	Lobster stew
Cloïsses	Clams, often steamed
Espinagada de Sa Pobla	Turnover filled with spinach and eel
Greixonera de peix	Menorcan fish stew, cooked in a pottery casserole
Guisat de peix	Fish and shellfish stew
Llagosta (amb pollastre)	Lobster (with chicken in a rich sauce)
Lluç	Hake, either fried or grilled
Musclos al vapor	Steamed mussels
Pop	Octopus
Rap a l'all cremat	Monkfish with creamed garlic sauce
Sarsuela	Fish and shellfish stew
Suquet	Fish casserole
Tonyina	Tuna
Truita	Trout (sometimes stuffed with ham, a la Navarre)

DESSERTS (POSTRES) AND PASTRIES (PASTAS)

Cocaroll	Pastry containing vegetables and fish
Crema Catalana	Crème caramel, with caramelized sugar topping
Ensaimada	Flaky spiral pastry with fillings such as cabello de ángel (sweetened citron rind)
Mel i mató	Curd cheese and honey
Panades sobrasada	Pastry with peas, meat or fish
Postres de músic	Cake of dried fruit and nuts
Turrón	Almond fudge
Xurros	Deep-fried doughnut sticks (served with hot chocolate)

LANGUAGE Food and drink

LANGUAGE

Food and drink

Drinking

ENGLISH	CATALAN	CASTILIAN
Water	Aigua	Agua
Mineral water	Aigua mineral	Agua mineral
(sparkling)	(amb gas)	(con gas)
(still)	(sense gas)	(sin gas)
Milk	Llet	Leche
Juice	Suc	Zumo
Tiger nut drink	Orxata	Horchata
Coffee	Café	Café
Espresso	Café sol	Café solo
White coffee	Café amb llet	Café con leche
Decaff	Descafeinat	Descafeinado
Tea	Te	Té
Drinking chocolate	Xocolata	Chocolate
Beer	Cervesa	Cerveza
Wine	Vi	Vino
Champagne/	Xampan/Cava	Champán/Cava
Sparkling wine		

Advertiser

ROUGH GUIDES TRAVEL...

UK & Ireland

Britain
Devon & Cornwall
Dublin
Edinburgh
England
Ireland
Lake District
London
London
  DIRECTIONS
London Mini Guide
Scotland
Scottish Highlands
  & Islands
Wales

Europe

Algarve
Amsterdam
Amsterdam
  DIRECTIONS
Andalucía
Athens DIRECTIONS
Austria
Baltic States
Barcelona
Belgium &
  Luxembourg
Berlin
Brittany &
  Normandy
Bruges & Ghent
Brussels
Budapest
Bulgaria
Copenhagen
Corfu
Corsica
Costa Brava
Crete
Croatia
Cyprus
Czech & Slovak
  Republics
Dodecanese & East
  Aegean
Dordogne & The Lot
Europe
Florence
France

Germany
Greece
Greek Islands
Hungary
Ibiza & Formentera
Iceland
Ionian Islands
Italy
Languedoc &
  Roussillon
Lisbon
Lisbon DIRECTIONS
The Loire
Madeira
Madrid
Mallorca
Malta & Gozo
Menorca
Moscow
Netherlands
Norway
Paris
Paris DIRECTIONS
Paris Mini Guide
Poland
Portugal
Prague
Provence & the
  Côte d'Azur
Pyrenees
Romania
Rome
Sardinia
Scandinavia
Sicily
Slovenia
Spain
St Petersburg
Sweden
Switzerland
Tenerife & La
  Gomera
Tenerife
  DIRECTIONS
Turkey
Tuscany & Umbria
Venice & The
  Veneto
Venice DIRECTIONS
Vienna

Asia

Bali & Lombok
Bangkok
Beijing
Cambodia
China
Goa
Hong Kong &
  Macau
India
Indonesia
Japan
Laos
Malaysia, Singapore
  & Brunei
Nepal
Philippines
Singapore
South India
Southeast Asia
Sri Lanka
Thailand
Thailand's Beaches
  & Islands
Tokyo
Vietnam

Australasia

Australia
Melbourne
New Zealand
Sydney

North America

Alaska
Big Island of Hawaii
Boston
California
Canada
Chicago
Florida
Grand Canyon
Hawaii
Honolulu
Las Vegas
Los Angeles
Maui
Miami & the Florida
  Keys
Montréal

New England
New Orleans
New York City
New York City
  DIRECTIONS
New York City Mini
  Guide
Pacific Northwest
Rocky Mountains
San Francisco
San Francisco
  DIRECTIONS
Seattle
Southwest USA
Toronto
USA
Vancouver
Washington DC
Yosemite

Caribbean
& Latin America

Antigua & Barbuda
Antigua
  DIRECTIONS
Argentina
Bahamas
Barbados
Barbados
  DIRECTIONS
Belize
Bolivia
Brazil
Caribbean
Central America
Chile
Costa Rica
Cuba
Dominican Republic
Ecuador
Guatemala
Jamaica
Maya World
Mexico
Peru
St Lucia
South America
Trinidad & Tobago

Rough Guides are available from good bookstores worldwide. New titles ar
published every month. Check www.roughguides.com for the latest news.

...MUSIC & REFERENCE

Africa & Middle East
Cape Town
Egypt
The Gambia
Jordan
Kenya
Marrakesh
  DIRECTIONS
Morocco
South Africa,
  Lesotho &
  Swaziland
Syria
Tanzania
Tunisia
West Africa
Zanzibar
Zimbabwe

Travel Theme guides
First-Time Around
  the World
First-Time Asia
First-Time Europe
First-Time Latin
  America
Skiing &
  Snowboarding in
  North America
Travel Online
Travel Health
Walks in London &
  SE England
Women Travel

Restaurant guides
French Hotels &
  Restaurants
London
New York
San Francisco

Maps
Algarve
Amsterdam
Andalucia & Costa
  del Sol

Argentina
Athens
Australia
Baja California
Barcelona
Berlin
Boston
Brittany
Brussels
Chicago
Crete
Croatia
Cuba
Cyprus
Czech Republic
Dominican
  Republic
Dubai & UAE
Dublin
Egypt
Florence & Siena
Frankfurt
Greece
Guatemala & Belize
Iceland
Ireland
Kenya
Lisbon
London
Los Angeles
Madrid
Mexico
Miami & Key West
Morocco
New York City
New Zealand
Northern Spain
Paris
Peru
Portugal
Prague
Rome
San Francisco
Sicily
South Africa
South India
Sri Lanka
Tenerife
Thailand
Toronto

Trinidad & Tobago
Tuscany
Venice
Washington DC
Yucatán Peninsula

Dictionary Phrasebooks
Czech
Dutch
Egyptian Arabic
European
  Languages
  (Czech, French,
  German,
  Greek, Italian,
  Portuguese,
  Spanish)
French
German
Greek
Hindi & Urdu
Hungarian
Indonesian
Italian
Japanese
Mandarin Chinese
Mexican Spanish
Polish
Portuguese
Russian
Spanish
Swahili
Thai
Turkish
Vietnamese

Music Guides
The Beatles
Bob Dylan
Cult Pop
Classical Music
Country Music
Elvis
Hip Hop
House
Irish Music
Jazz
Music USA
Opera

Reggae
Rock
Techno
World Music (2
  vols)

History Guides
China
Egypt
England
France
India
Islam
Italy
Spain
USA

Reference Guides
Books for
  Teenagers
Children's Books,
  0–5
Children's Books,
  5–11
Cult Fiction
Cult Football
Cult Movies
Cult TV
Ethical Shopping
Formula 1
The iPod, iTunes &
  Music Online
The Internet
Internet Radio
James Bond
Kids' Movies
Lord of the Rings
Muhammed Ali
Man Utd
Personal
  Computers
Pregnancy & Birth
Shakespeare
Superheroes
Unexplained
  Phenomena
The Universe
Videogaming
Weather
Website Directory

Also! More than 120 Rough Guide music CDs are available from all good book and record stores. Listen in at www.worldmusic.net

ROUGH GUIDE MAPS

Printed on waterproof and rip-proof Polyart™ paper, offering an unbeatable combination of practicality, clarity of design and amazing value.

ROUGH GUIDES
REFERENCE SERIES

  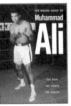

DON'T JUST TRAVEL!

ROUGH GUIDES
TRAVEL SERIES

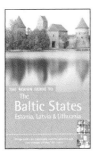

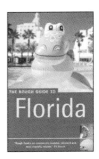

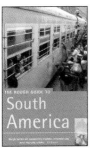

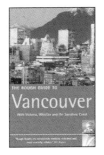

**Travel guides to more than 250
destinations
from Alaska to Zimbabwe**

smooth travel

small print & Index

SMALL PRINT

A Rough Guide to Rough Guides

Mallorca DIRECTIONS is published by Rough Guides. The first *Rough Guide to Greece*, published in 1982, was a student scheme that became a publishing phenomenon. The immediate success of the book – with numerous reprints and a Thomas Cook prize short-listing – spawned a series that rapidly covered dozens of destinations. Rough Guides had a ready market among low-budget backpackers, but soon also acquired a much broader and older readership that relished Rough Guides' wit and inquisitiveness as much as their enthusiastic, critical approach. Everyone wants value for money, but not at any price. Rough Guides soon began supplementing the "rougher" information about hostels and low-budget listings with the kind of detail on restaurants and quality hotels that independent-minded visitors on any budget might expect, whether on business in New York or trekking in Thailand. These days the guides offer recommendations from shoestring to luxury and cover a large number of destinations around the globe, including almost every country in the Americas and Europe, more than half of Africa and most of Asia and Australasia. Rough Guides now publish:

- Travel guides to more than 200 worldwide destinations
- Dictionary phrasebooks to 22 major languages
- Maps printed on rip-proof and waterproof Polyart™ paper
- Music guides running the gamut from Opera to Elvis
- Reference books on topics as diverse as the Weather and Shakespeare
- World Music CDs in association with World Music Network

Publishing information

This 1st edition published May 2005 by
Rough Guides Ltd, 80 Strand, London WC2R 0RL;
345 Hudson St, 4th Floor, New York, NY 10014, USA.

Distributed by the Penguin Group
Penguin Books Ltd, 80 Strand, London WC2R 0RL
Penguin Group (USA), 375 Hudson Street, New York, NY 10014, USA
Penguin Group (Australia), 487 Maroondah Highway, PO Box 257, Ringwood, Victoria 3134, Australia
Penguin Group (Canada), 10 Alcorn Avenue, Toronto, Ontario M4V 1E4, Canada
Penguin Group (NZ), 182–190 Wairau Road, Auckland 10, New Zealand
Typeset in Bembo and Helvetica to an original design by Henry Iles.
Printed and bound in China by Leo

A catalogue record for this book is available from the British Library.

ISBN 1-84353-453-3

The publishers and authors have done their best to ensure the accuracy and currency of all the information in **Mallorca DIRECTIONS**. However, they can accept no responsibility for any loss, injury, or inconvenience sustained by any traveller as a result of information or advice contained in the guide.

1   3   5   7   9   8   6   4   2

Help us update

We've gone to a lot of effort to ensure that the first edition of **Mallorca DIRECTIONS** is accurate and up to date. However, things change – places get "discovered", opening hours are notoriously fickle, restaurants and rooms raise prices or lower standards. If you feel we've got it wrong or left something out, we'd like to know, and if you can remember the address, the price, the phone number, so much the better.

We'll credit all contributions, and send a copy of the next edition (or any other DIRECTIONS guide or Rough Guide if you prefer) for the best letters. Everyone who writes to us and isn't already a subscriber will receive a copy of our full-colour thrice-yearly newsletter. Please mark letters: **"Mallorca DIRECTIONS Update"** and send to: Rough Guides, 80 Strand, London WC2R 0RL, or Rough Guides, 4th Floor, 345 Hudson St, New York, NY 10014. Or send an email to **mail@roughguides.com**

Have your questions answered and tell others about your trip at **www.roughguides.atinfopop.com**

Rough Guide credits

Text editors: Lucy Ratcliffe, Helena Smith
Layout: Andy Hilliard
Photography: Ian Aitken
Cartography: Jai Prakash Mishra
Picture editor: Eleanor Hill

Proofreader: Diane Margolis
Production: Julia Bovis
Design: Henry Iles
Cover art direction: Chloe Roberts

The author

Phil Lee has worked as a freelance author with Rough Guides for over ten years. Previous titles include the Rough Guides to Menorca, Belgium & Luxembourg, Amsterdam and Norway. He lives in Nottingham, where he was born and raised.

Acknowledgements

Phil would like to thank the following for their especially helpful letters and emails: Alison Ewington; Felisa Forteza; Nicola Hambridge; Elizabeth Key; Beverley Lawe; Peter Lloyd; Karin von Herrath Ross; Zelda Tolley; Janet Trapmore; Joana Vives; Stephanie Webb; M. Welch; Stephen Withers; and Claire Woodward. Thanks also to Lucy Ratcliffe for her careful editing, Eleanor Hill for picture research, Andy Hilliard for layout, Jai Prakashmishra for maps and Ian Aitken for photography.

Photo credits

All images © Rough Guides except the following:

p.48 Street scene, Palma © Simon Bracken
p.11 Monastir de Lluc © Ditta U. Krebs/Fotostock Mallorca
p.16 Corpus Christi, Sóller © Ditta U. Krebs/Fotostock Mallorca
p.16 Moors and Christians, Sóller © Ditta U. Krebs/Fotostock Mallorca
p.17 Revelta de Sant Antoni Abat, Sóller © Ditta U. Krebs/Fotostock Mallorca
p.17 Carnival (Carnaval) – February, Palma © David Seri
p.17 Holy Week – Setmana Santa, Palma © David Seri
p.17 Escolania de Lluc – Choir boys at Lluc Monastery © Ditta U. Krebs/Fotostock Mallorca
p.20 Tito's © David Seri
p.21 Pacha, Palma © www.dilmy.com
p.21 DJ at festival © David Seri
p.24 Hoopoe © Gordon Langsbury/rspb-images.com
p.24 Purple Gallinule © Carlos Sanchez/rspb-images.com
p.25 Black Vulture © Carlos Sanchez/rspb-images.com
p.25 Audoin's Gull © Marianne Wilding/rspb-images.com
p.28 Chipirones, prepared, beach bar at Cala Argulla © Ditta U. Krebs/Fotostock Mallorca
p.29 Mallorcan sausage shop, Palma © Ditta U. Krebs/Fotostock Mallorca
p.30 Francesc Comes, El Salvador S XV, Iglesia de Santa Eulalia © Oronoz
p.31 Master of Montesión: Retablo de Escuela Mallorquina, aka 'Retablo De Nuestra Señora De Montesió', Colegio/Conv Montesio © Oronoz
p.33 Mondragó beach © Simon Bracken
p.38 Festa des Verema, Binissalem. Photo 2004. © Ditta U. Krebs/Fotostock, Mallorca
p.44 Snorkelling, Puerto de Sóller © Ditta U. Krebs/Fotostock, Mallorca
p.45 Windsurfing © David Seri

Index

Map entries are marked in colour

A

accommodation 155
airport, Mallorca 151
Alaró 92
Alcúdia 116
Alcúdia 116
Alfabia, Jardins d' 90
Algaida 128
Andratx 100
Anglada–Camarasa, Hermen 64
Aquacity 40, 76
Aquapark 41, 79
arrival 151
Artà 132
Artà caves 19, 135
ATMs 158
auto rental 154

B

Bacon, Francis 97
Badia de Palma 74–85
Badia de Palma 75
Balearic cuisine 28–29, 170
Banyalbufar 99
Bardolet, José Coll 110
bars
  Abaco 71, 21
  Barcelona Jazz Café Club 72
  Taberna La Bovéda 72
Bay of Palma 74–85
Bay of Palma 75
beaches 32–33, 156
Betlem, Ermita de 133
bicycling 154, 156
Biniaraix 88
Binissalem 38–39, 92
birdlife 24–25
birdwatching 24–25, 43, 119
bocadillos 169
Bonaire 117
Bonany, Ermita de Nostra Senyora de 130
Botanicactus 141
Bunyola 91
buses, Bay of Palma 74
buses, Mallorcan 153, 154
buses, Southern Mallorca 125
buses, to Sóller 86

C

Cabrera island 144
cafés
  Bar Bosch 68
  Bon Lloc 69
  La Bóveda 69
  Ca'n Joan de S'Aigo 69
  Cappuccino 69
  La Cueva 70
  Lizarran 70
  El Pesquero 70
  El Pilon 70
Cala Agulla, Platja (Cala Rajada) 134
Cala Bona 135
Cala Deià 33, 93
Cala d'Or 139
Cala Estellencs 32, 100
Cala Figuera 140
Cala Figuera, Cap de 80
Cala Fornells 81
Cala Gat (Cala Rajada) 134
Cala Gran 139
Cala Llonga
Cala Mago 80
Cala Major 76
Cala Marçal 138
Cala Millor 135
Cala Mondragó 33, 45, 140
Cala Rajada 133
Cala Sant Vicenç 114
Cala Santanyí 140
Cala Tuent 108
Calderers, Els 131
Calvià 79
Camp de Mar 82
Cap Blanc 145
Cap de Capdepera 134
Cap de Formentor 25, 43, 115
Cap de Ses Salines 141
Capdepera 18, 134
Capdepera, Cap de 134
Capocorb Vell 23, 145
car rental 154
Castell d'Alaró 19, 91
Castell de Santueri 19, 139
Castilian 5, 163–172
Catalan 5, 163–172
Cathedral, Palma 10, 14, 51
caves 19, 135, 136, 137
cell phones 158
children in Mallorca 158
choir, boys', Escolania de Lluc 17, 109
Chopin, Frédéric 97

climate 6
clubs 20–21
Colònia de Sant Jordi 141
Colònia de Sant Jordi 142–143
Cornadors Circuit 88
Costa dels Pins 135
Cova Blava 144
Coves d'Artà 19, 135
Coves del Drac 136
Coves d'es Hams 137
Covetes, Ses 143
credit cards 158
Cúber reservoir 108
cuisine, Balearic 28–29, 170
cuisine, Mallorcan 28–29, 170
Cura, Santuari de Nostra Senyora de 15, 128
currency exchange 158
cycle rental 154
cycling 154, 156

D

Davallament, the 113
debit cards 158
Deià 11, 93
dentists 158
disabilities, travellers with 158
diving 156
DJ nights 20–21
doctors 158
Drac caves 136
drink glossaries, food and 167–172
drinks 172

E

electricity (current) 158
Els Calderers 131
email 158
Embalse de Cúber 108
emergencies 158
Ermita de Betlem 133
Ermita de Nostra Senyora de Bonany 130
Ermita de Nostra Senyora del Puig, Pollença 113
Ermita de Sant Miquel 129
Es Pla 125
Es Trenc 33, 142
Escolania de Lluc (boys' choir) 17, 109
Esporles 99

Estellencs 99
euro, the 158
exchange, currency 158
exchange rate 158

F

Felanitx 138
ferries to Mallorca 151
ferry terminal 152
festivals 16–17, 156–157
festivals, Port de Sóller 90
fincas 155
food and drink glossaries 167–172
Formentor peninsula 115
Fornalutx 89
Fundació Pilar i Joan Miró 46, 47, 77

G

Galilea 99
gardens, Alfàbia 90
gardens, botanical (Sóller) 88
gardens, botanical, Lluc 111
gardens, La Granja 98
Gaudí, Antoni 55
Glassworks, Gordiola 126
glossaries, food and drink 167–172
Gordiola Glassworks 126
Gorg Blau 43, 107
La Granja 98
Graves, Robert 93, 94

H

Hams caves 137
Hidropark 41, 118
hiking 156
hiking maps 153
holidays, public 157
horse riding 156
hostals – see Hotels
hotels by area
   Bay of Palma 82–83
   Northern Mallorca 121–122
   Palma 67–68
   Southern Mallorca 145–146
   Western Mallorca 102–103
hotels
   Apuntadores 67
   Bahía 121
   Bon Sol 82
   Born 68, 35
   Brondo 67
   Ca's Bombu 145

Ca's Xorc 102, 37
Cala Fornells 82
Can Llenaire 121
Casa Chiquita 145
Convent de la Missió 68
Coronado 82
Costa d'Or, Llucalcari 102, 37
Cuba 67
Dalt Murada 68
Es Convent 121
Es Molí 102
Es Turó 145
Felip 146
Formentor 121, 36
El Guía 102, 12, 35
Juma 122
L'Hermitage 103
Leon de Sineu 146
Marina 103
Miramar 102
Nixe Palace 83
Palacio Ca Sa Galesa 68
Petit 103
Playa 145
Playa Esperanza 122
Portixol 83, 34
Posada de Lluc 122
Ritzi 67
Santuari de la Victòria 121
Saratoga 68, 34
Scott's Binissalem 103, 35
Scott's Galilea 103, 37
Ses Rotges 146
Sis Pins 122
Sol Jaime III 68
Son Sant Jordi 122
Villa Verde 103
hotels, last minute at the airport 151

I

Illetes 78
information offices in Mallorca 152
Internet 152, 158
Internet cafés 158

J

Jardí Botànic (Sóller) 87
Jardins d'Alfàbia 90
jet skiing 45, 156

K

kids' Mallorca 40–41

L

La Granja 98
language 5, 163–172
Les Meravelles 76
Lilfords wall lizard 144
Lladó, J. Torrents 58
Lluc monastery 11, 109
Llucmajor 145

M

Magaluf 79
mail 158
majolica 110
Mallorca airport 151
Mallorcan cuisine 28–29, 170
Mallorcan Primitives (painters) 30–31, 55, 59, 62
Manacor 15, 131
maps 153
maps, hiking 153
March, Banca, in Palma 65
March, Joan 56
Massanella, Puig de 108
medical emergencies 158
menu reader 167–172
Les Merravelles 76
Mirador de Ricardo Roca 100
Miró, Joan 46, 47, 77, 97
mobile phones 158
monastery accommodation
   Northern Mallorca 121–122
   Southern Mallorca 145–146
monastery, Valldemossa 11, 47, 97
Mondragó Parc Natural 24, 42, 140
Monestir de Lluc 11, 109
Montuïri 128
moped rental 155
Muro 119

N

Northern Mallorca 106–124
Northern Mallorca 106–107

O

opening hours 158
Orient 91

P

pa amb oli 29, 170

Palma 51–73
  Ajuntament 63
  Art Espanyol Contemporani, Museu d' 65, 47
  Avinguda Jaume III 63
  Banca March 65
  Banys Àrabs 58
  bars 71
  bars, tapas 68
  Basílica de Sant Francesc 61, 14
  buses 54
  cafés 68
  Can Oleza 59
  Can Rei 65
  Can Solleric 63
  Can Vivot 59
  Castell de Bellver 66, 19
  Cathedral 51–55, 10, 14
  Consolat de Mar 66
  drinking 68
  eating 68
  Es Baluard 66, 46
  Forn des Teatre 64
  Fundació La Caixa 64
  Gaudí, Antoni 55
  Gran Hotel 64
  harbourfront 66
  hostals 67
  hotels 67
  information 54
  Jaume III, Avinguda 63
  L'Àguila 65
  Lladó, J Torrents 58
  Mallorcan Primitives (painters) 55, 30–31, 59, 62
  mansions in Palma, Renaissance 60
  March, Banca 65
  March, Joan 56
  March, Palau Museu 56, 47
  Monti-Sion, church of 62
  Museu d'Art Espanyol Contemporani 65, 47
  Museu de la Catedral 55
  Museu de Mallorca 58
  Museu Diocesà 62
  Museu J Torrents Lladó 58
  orientation 54
  Palau de l'Almudaina 55
  Palau March Museu 56, 47
  Parc de la Mar 56, 21
  Passeig d'es Born 63
  Passeig Mallorca 66
  Plaça Cort 63
  Plaça Major 65
  Plaça Marques del Palmer 65
  Plaça Mercat 64
  Plaça Sant Jeroni 61
  Plaça Weyler 64
  Portella 57
  Primitives, Mallorcan (painters) 30–31, 55, 59 , 62
  restaurants 70
  Sa Llotja 66
  Sant Francesc, Basílica de 61, 14
  Sant Jeroni, church of 61
  Santa Eulalia, church of 60, 15
  Serra, Junípero 61
  shopping 72
  tapas bars 68
  Teatre Principal 64
  trains to Sóller 86
  transport, city 54
  walls, city 56
Palma Nova 78
Palma, Bay of 74–85
Palma, Bay of 75
Palma, Central 52–53
Parc Natural de S'Albufera 24, 25, 43, 119
Parc Natural, Mondragó 24, 42, 140
parks, water & theme 40–41
passports 159
Peguera 81
Península de Formentor 25, 115
Penya Roja 118
Petra 129
phones 159
Platja Cala Agulla (Cala Rajada) 134
Platja Cala Comtesa 78
Platja de Formentor 115
Platja de Palma 33, 76
Platja Son Moll (Cala Rajada) 134
Pollença 111
Pollença 112
Pollentia 22, 117
Port d'Alcúdia 32, 118
Port d'Andratx 101
Port de Pollença 114
Port de Sóller 44, 89
Port de Valldemossa 98
Portals Nous 40, 78
Portals Vells 80
Porto Colom 138
Porto Cristo 136
Porto Cristo 137
Porto Petro 140
post 158
Primitives, Mallorcan (painters) 30–31, 55, 59, 62
public holidays 157
Puig d'es Teix 93
Puig de l'Àguila 114
Puig de Massanella 108
Puig Major 107, 108
Puig Randa 128
Puigpunyent 99

R

racions 169
Ramís, Juli 47, 97
Real Cartuja, Valldemossa 11, 47, 97
restaurants by area
  Bay of Palma 83
  Northern Mallorca 123–124
  Palma 70–71
  Southern Mallorca 146–147
  Western Mallorca 103–105
restaurants
  Aramís 70
  Asador Tierra Aranda 70
  Ca'n Balaguer 146
  Ca'n Carlos 71, 13
  Ca'n Mario 103, 13
  Ca'n Simo 123
  Caballito del Mar 71
  Café Parisien 146
  Cantonet 123
  Celler Es Grop 146
  Es Canyís 104
  Es Faro 104
  Es Parlament 71, 12
  Es Port 104
  Es Racó d'es Teix 104, 13
  Es Reco de Randa 147
  Flamingo 147
  Flanagan's 83
  Flor de Loto 71
  Florian 147
  Forn de Sant Joan 71
  Fragua, La 147
  Galicia 105
  Gran Tortuga, La 83
  Il Giardino 123
  Ivy Garden 123
  Jaime 105
  Juma 123
  Mangiafuoco 71
  Méson Ca'n Torrat
  Mirador de la Victòria 123
  Pizzeria Roma 123
  Port Blau 147
  El Puerto 147
  Sa Cova 105
  Sa Dorada 105
  Sa Plaça 124
  Ses Porxeres 105
  Ses Rotges 147
  Stay 124
  Tristan 83
Ribas, Antoni 110
Roman ruins of Pollentia 22, 117
Roman Theatre 23, 117

S

Sa Calobra 108
Sa Coma 136
Sa Dragonera 42, 100
Sa Foradada 95
Sa Pobla 120
sailing 156
S'Albufera, Parc Natural de 24, 25, 43, 119
Salines de Llevant 143

Salvator, Ludwig 94
Sand, George 97
Sant Elm 100
Sant Miquel, Ermita de 129
Sant Salvador, Santuari
  de 138
Santa Catalina Thomàs 95
Santa Ponça 81
Santanyí 140
Santuari de la Victòria 117
Santuari de Nostra Senyora de
  Cura 15, 128
Santuari de Sant Salvador 138
S'Arenal 76
Serra de Tramuntana 11,
  43, 106
Serra, Junípero 61, 129
Serres de Llevant 125,
  132, 133
Ses Covetes 143
Ses Paisses 22, 132
S'Illot 136
shops by area
  Bay of Palma 83
  Northern Mallorca 124
  Palma 72–73
  Western Mallorca 105
shops
  Alcúdia market 124
  Bennassar Galleries 124
  Bodega de José Luis
    Ferrer 105
  La Bodeguilla 73
  Ca'n Matarino 105
  Camper 72
  Carnisseria Mary Carmen 148
  Casa del Mapa 72

  Casa del Olivo 72
  Casa del Vino 148, 39
  Ceramiques de Santanyí 148
  Colmado Santo Domingo 72
  El Corte Inglés 72
  Ensenat 124
  Finca Gourmet 105
  Forn Fondo 72
  Fundació Pilar i Joan Miró 83
  Gordiola Glassworks 148
  Libreria Calabruix 105
  Majorica 73
  Sineu market 148
  Vidrias Gordiola 73
Sineu 15, 129
Sóller 86–88
Sóller 87
Sóller train 10, 86
Sóller tunnel 86
Sometimes 76
Son Marroig 94
Southern Mallorca 125–148
Southern Mallorca 126–127
Spanish language 163–172
sports 44–45
Sureda, Bartomeu 110

theme parks 40–41
Thomàs, Santa Catalina 95
time zone 159
Torrent de Pareis 109
tourist offices in Mallorca 152
trains to Sóller 10, 86
trains, Mallorcan 11, 154
trains, Southern Mallorca 125
trams, Port de Sóller 86
transport, Mallorcan 153
tunnel to Sóller 86

T

tapas 169
tapas bars, see cafés
Teatre Romà 23, 117
Teix, Puig d'es 93
telephones 159
temperatures 6

V

Valldemossa 11, 47, 95–97
Valldemossa 96
Vernes, Jules 135
Villalonga, Llorenç 92
visas 159

W

walking maps 153
water parks 40–41
watersports 44–45
weather 6
websites, useful 152
Western Mallorca 84–105
Western Mallorca 84–85
Western Water Park 41, 79
windsurfing 156, 45

DATE DUE

HIGHSMITH 45231